Enjoy!

Best,

Bill

RETIRE IN A WEEKEND!

*"Your 'I can't guarantee squat!' mantra is AWESOME!
This truth will set millions of baby boomer's free!"*
~ Leo J. Quinn Jr., ·
author of *How To Own Your Paycheck Again*

"Bill Losey has broken from the pack of books on retirement with this most readable, light hearted, but information-packed guide to retirement investing. His humorous style mixed with hard data gives the readers exactly what they need to feel good about their retirement finances. This is the only retirement financial book you'll ever need."
~ Richard P. Johnson, Ph.D.,
President, Retirement Options, Inc.

"Retire in a Weekend! is a must read for every baby boomer with assets to protect. Bill Losey's '1% Solution' is a sound concept whose time has come and all Americans should embrace".
~ Kevin Johnson,
President, National Long-Term Care Brokers

"In the vast world of financial planners, Bill Losey is a breath of fresh air. He understands that most of us are on entirely different pages when it comes to retirement, and a one-size-fits-all approach just doesn't work. Retire in a Weekend! is the most refreshing, informative, unusual book on retirement...ever!"
~ Lin Schreiber,
President, Revolutionize Retirement™

"The information Bill presents on investing, specifically how market efficiency and costs matter, was a real eye opener. People could enhance their investing performance and save thousands or tens of thousands of dollars over their lifetime by implementing a portfolio that combines actively and passively managed investments. Smart move!"
~ Jeffrey M. Many, CPA

PRAISE FOR RETIRE IN A WEEKEND!

"Baby boomers are quickly realizing that they must control their lives and now their retirement. Bill makes a complex issue easy and fun to understand and empowers you to take control of your own retirement. This is a must read book for everyone."

~ David Neagle,
President, Life is Now Inc. & author of *The Art of Success*

"I hate financial talk. But when I read Bill's 'Safe Money' Benchmark Strategy I felt this huge weight lift off of my shoulders. Brilliant and simple. Enjoying a long and prosperous retirement never looked so doable."

~ Valerie Young,
Dreamer in Residence, ChangingCourse.com

"Bill reveals a proven system to help you fine-tune your portfolio and bolster your nest egg so that you can easily and safely realize your retirement dream much sooner than much later. In fact, you may be able to start living your retirement dream the day you complete reading this book!"

~ Ernie J. Zelinski,
author of the international bestseller
How to Retire, Happy, Wild, and Free

"Every baby boomer should eat right, exercise and read Retire in a Weekend! *Bill Losey is just what the doctor ordered to improve your wealth and happiness!"*

~ Dr. Bryan Briddell,
President, Total Fitness Solution, LLC

"Bill's commentary on how our relationships affect retirement success or failure is a must read! Every baby boomer, woman and couple needs Retire in a Weekend!*"*

~Dr. Cindy Brown,
Behavior Specialist & Author of *The Cinderella System - 7 Steps to Attracting the Man & Relationship of Your Dreams*

RETIRE IN A WEEKEND!

"Bill Losey's book, Retire in a Weekend! *is a rare find that expertly integrates quality of life issues with outstanding financial advice."*
~ James Lange, CPA/JD,
author *Retire Secure!*

"Bill has explained complex financial issues in a clear, witty, and very understandable manner. Retire in a Weekend! *is a timely book for we baby boomers known for our 'alternative ways' of approaching life!"*
~Helen Harlow,
Executive Senior Sales Director, Mary Kay Cosmetics

"I'm amazed at the myth-busting humor Bill Losey brings to the -- for some of us -- scary topic of retirement finances. There are many books on the subject, but you should read Retire in a Weekend! *first. It calms fears and clears up bewilderment. All you may ever need to know about money in later life is there."*
~ David Savageau,
author, *Retirement Places Rated*

"Bill Losey's easy-to-read, fun, and thought-provoking book skillfully guides you through the maze of retirement options to help you develop a focused plan in a single weekend – one that will propel you forward to achieve your financial dreams and live your life with freedom, passion and purpose."
~Lauren E. Sullivan,
life coach and author of *Give Wings to Your Dreams: Reawaken Your Joy and Passion for Life*

"Very readable and valuable information about the 'moving target' of financial planning for retirement years. Bill's frequently reinforced notion that 'I can't guarantee squat!' as an investment planner is worth its weight in gold. Good stuff!"
~ Jeff Thredgold, CSP,
economic futurist and author of *econAmerica, Why the American Economy is Alive and Well...And What That Means to Your Wallet*

PRAISE FOR RETIRE IN A WEEKEND!

"This book is for the straight-shooters of the world – those that want to know the REAL deal about their retirement. Bill trades in the gobbledygook for simple strategies. YEA!!"

~ Vickie Sullivan,
President, Sullivan Speaker Services, Inc.

"As a leading edge baby boomer (60+), I found Bill's book easy to read and extremely relevant. Bill points out that he sometimes feels like 'a motivational speaker, pastor, and psychologist all at the same time…' He's that and more. I would add – down to earth, straight-talking, with a great sense of humor. If you are a baby boomer and have any concerns about your retirement, I highly recommend Retire in a Weekend!*"*

~ Tom Manfredi,
Author of the baby boomer fitness site
– www.fitness-after-50.com

"Bill shares a lightly written, upbeat guide for people considering retirement. His presentation shares lots to consider without overwhelming the reader. It's a quick read, written in lay terms that is very hands-on and packed with informational gems."

~ Dotsie Bregel,
Founder, National Association of
Baby Boomer Women, www.nabbw.com

"Regardless of your age, occupation, or income level, Retire in a Weekend! *is a must read if you're looking to retire someday and enjoy the fruits of your hard labor."*

~ Todd Durkin, MA, CSCS, NCTMB
Owner, Fitness Quest 10 & Todd Durkin Enterprises
2 Time Personal Trainer of the Year

RETIRE IN A WEEKEND!

"For many folks, retirement planning is scary, unpredictable and totally baffling. With clarity, passion and wit, Bill Losey brilliantly demystifies how to create a retirement that's just perfect for you. Retire in a Weekend! *is a definite must-read book that will help you become the master of your destiny!"*

~ Carolyn B. Ellis,
Author of *The 7 Pitfalls of Single Parenting* and
Founder of ThriveAfterDivorce.com

*"*Retire in a Weekend! *is quick, easy and to the point…it gives life to your thoughts and dreams. It's a hole in one!"*

~ Charles Davis,
Co-Host, The Golf Channel's "Grey Goose 19th Hole"

"Are you ready to design and live the life that you desire? Retire in a Weekend! *provides a clear blueprint to get you the results you want!"*

~ Diana Long,
Founder & President, The Life Design Institute LLC

"Unlike most books on personal finance that are long, dry and boring, Retire in a Weekend! *is short, easy-to-understand, and laced with humor. Bill Losey's wit and wisdom about retirement investing, creating an income for life, and happiness is priceless!"*

~ Steve Nussbaum,
President, Nussbaum Long-Term Care
Planning & Insurance

"We don't understand a word of this book, but our dad worked hard on it all summer and mom says its real good despite his corny sense of humor. Please buy Retire in a Weekend! *so we can afford to go to college someday."*

~ Tyler, Connor & Andrew Losey,
the author's three sons

RETIRE
IN A
WEEKEND!

The Baby Boomer's Guide
to Making Work Optional

Do what you want, when you want, where you want.

AMERICA'S RETIREMENT STRATEGIST™
BILL LOSEY, CFP, CSA
WWW.MYRETIREMENTSUCCESS.COM

Retire in a Weekend!
The Baby Boomer's Guide to Making Work Optional

Published by:
Love Your Life Publishing
PO Box 2, Dallastown, PA 17313
www.LoveYourLife.com

ISBN: 978-0-9798554-1-2

Library of Congress Control No: 2007939110

Cover design, layout and typesetting by Sarah Van Male, Cyanotype Book Architects.

Printed in the United States of America

 Printed on recycled paper.

Table of Contents

Foreword

Remember that old song? The words that resonate for me are...you make my heart sing. Take a moment, maybe even close your eyes and get a visceral hit of that. Say over and over, "If my heart could sing, what would it be saying? Would it sing at the top of its lungs with happiness; or would it be subdued and soft? What would the words be?"

I contend that few of us even know what makes our heart sing. You know, so many of us spend yeeeaaars...doing for others, or doing what others want us to do. We bury our own desires as we live our busy lives of raising families, building careers, etc. Well, you know what? Today is the day to reckon with that and go for what you truly want!

It's time to live your life on your terms...and there are 3 simple rules for doing that:

1. Stop doing what you DON'T want to do.
2. Start doing what you DO want to do.

3. Don't let anyone else tell you what you CAN'T or SHOULDN'T do.

So, how does all this fit in with Bill Losey's wonderful book: *Retire in a Weekend!*?

Well, Bill shares with you from his heart and soul, what it will take for you to live life on your terms, to make your heart sing! In this jam-packed book, full of ideas and questions and FUN, Bill inspires you to take risks that are holding you back from doing what you really want to do. The same risks he took to walk away from a six-figure income, start his own home-based business, publish the world's largest collection of "blank" books, gather up the courage to sing in public, and eventually sing the National Anthem before 10,000+ fans at Madison Square Garden!

It's time to take your dreams out, dust them off and make them happen! Want to live elsewhere; start your own business; travel to distant places; form a non-profit, or become an artist? Whatever you want to do, this book will help you figure out how to make it happen.

Final thought: Every time you deny yourself, a little piece of your spirit dies! Don't deny yourself and those longings anymore, but rather, read *Retire in a Weekend!* and begin to really live a life full of fulfillment, richness and FUN!

~ Ann Fry, CEO, Head Boomer, ItsBoomerTime.com

FAQ - Read This First!

Here are some common doubts and fears people have before taking the leap and retiring:

Q - Do I need a pension to be able to retire comfortably?
A - No. While it is a little more challenging without one, more than 70% of my private clients rely solely on their savings, investments and social security. How do you create a predictable income for life? It's all here.

Q - Do I need a million dollars to retire comfortably?
A - Not at all. While accumulating a seven figure portfolio is a goal for many baby boomers, it isn't the 'end all - be all'. It all depends on the kind of lifestyle you desire. Frankly, if you're sick of hearing you need to be a multi-millionaire to retire, this book is for you.

Q - I love what I do. Should I retire?
A - Absolutely not! If you love what you do, you aren't "working", you're "playing". This is the zone everyone should be in regardless of their age or net worth. Plus, the longer you generate an income, the less you'll need to save.

Q - I just want more time. Do I have to retire?
A - No. Retiring is just one option. Through astute lifestyle and financial choices, you can have complete freedom today. My objective is to help you create the time you want, to use however you want.

Q - Unlike Michael Jordan, I only plan on retiring once and I'm afraid of making mistakes. Do I need to hire a professional to help me?
A - Nope. Plenty of folks do it themselves. However, if you feel you don't have the time, talent or temperament to go it alone, consider hiring a qualified advisor.

As a bonus, go to www.MyRetirementSuccess.com and click on the link for a "FREE 30-Page Report – The 10 Biggest Mistakes People Make When Retiring & How to Avoid Them". My FREE report will be emailed to you within a few moments and can alleviate some of your fears.

Why You Need to Read This Book

Stock markets stumble. Inflation is back. Pensions are dwindling. People retire earlier. Life lasts longer. Yadda, yadda, yadda.

> **What's the best age to retire?**

I don't think you should wait until you're 55, 60, 62 or 65 to retire. You can retire today!

Despite all the doom and gloom you hear about in the media, the scare tactics perpetuated by overly aggressive salesman, and advertising by some of the nations largest financial firms, millions of ordinary people – baby boomers like you and me – are making work optional, reinventing themselves, and enjoying extraordinary adventures right now.

I understand there are dozens of books on personal finance and retirement out there. In my research for this book, I learned most are too long, too technical, and filled with jargon. Some are too light and fluffy and woo-woo for my taste. So why read this book?

Retire in a Weekend! is different because it's based upon feedback from pre-retirees just like you. Over the past year I've surveyed my clients and hundreds of people who've attended my retirement and investing workshops, as well as thousands of subscribers to my free, award-winning newsletter, *Retirement Intelligence*™. My goal was to determine what your biggest retirement concerns were and what burning questions you wanted answered.

It didn't matter whether I was speaking with someone in New York or California, whether they were male or female, whether they had accumulated more or less than a million dollars, or if they were married, single, widowed or divorced, they all expressed the same concerns. After organizing and tabulating over 12,000 responses, five concerns and ten questions emerged over and over and over again. In the chapters that follow, this book will address all those questions and provide real world solutions.

Retirement Concerns*

Outliving my money – 38%
Failing/losing my health – 19%
Keeping up with inflation – 16%
Paying too much in taxes – 14%
Stock market volatility – 10%
Miscellaneous concerns – 3%

*Source: Bill Losey Retirement Solutions, LLC – 12,364 responses

---

I also listened intently as my seminar attendees expressed how they were confused and sometimes overwhelmed with all the conflicting financial information available. Most couldn't make sense of the overload of data. They didn't know what did or didn't matter to their situation, and they didn't know how to synthesize and apply it all. Most importantly, they were hungry for straight talk, not some fear-based sales pitch. I'll deliver on that request and provide simple examples and explanations.

I know I'm biased, but when it comes to *your* retirement, I believe *Retire in a Weekend!* will be the most important, eye-opening book, you will ever read on this topic. This is an extremely bold statement, but the bottom-line is, this book will give you the tools, confidence and know-how to never work another day in your life unless you choose to, rather than have to.

It is my belief that when you read and study this book, and you implement the strategies and *Retirement Success Principles* in it, you will transform your life and those of others around you.

In Part I of *Retire in a Weekend!*, I have compiled easy-to-understand answers addressing the most commonly asked questions I receive, as well as strategies to reduce or eliminate the biggest retirement concerns you may be feeling. I'll share with you the same *Retirement Success Principles* I implement with my private clients and illustrate what actions you can take today to ensure your best chance at retirement success tomorrow.

In Part II of *Retire in a Weekend!* I'll present some quick exercises you can complete that will open your mind and encourage you to explore life's possibilities and create the retirement you've always dreamed about! You'll discover (or rediscover) what you're truly passionate about and determine how you wish to invest your time, money and energy for the rest of your life.

As a fellow baby boomer, I know you're busy so I've intentionally kept the book short so that you could read it in a matter of hours over a weekend. It's a quick read.

There'll also be an occasional joke or two throughout. I like to laugh and have a good time, and am known for making the sometimes mundane and complicated topics of investing and retirement fun. I promise to keep it light. Enjoy!

Bill

Wanna good laugh right now?
*Go to **www.MyRetirementSuccess.com** and to the left side of the homepage, locate the headline **"The Baby Boomer Retirement Movie"**. Click the link that says "Watch Bill's 3-Minute Movie". Please allow 30 seconds for it to load.*

Acknowledgements

First, I want to thank the thousands of subscribers to my award-winning newsletter *Retirement Intelligence*™ and the hundreds of people who attended my retirement and investing workshops over the past year. Your feedback, questions and concerns birthed this book!

To my fellow Platinum Group coaching members, your support and encouragement propelled me faster than I was comfortable with. Thanks for the kick in the butt. Special kudos to Lucho Crisalle for suggesting the title, Dr. Cindy Brown for being my book buddy, and Christine Kloser for developing the "Get Your Book Done™" program. Without you Christine, this book would still be in my head. Also, special thanks to Lou Day for help with Chapter 5.

To my private clients, thanks so much for encouraging me, being excited for me, and giving me valuable feedback on my manuscript. I don't take our relationship for granted and greatly appreciate your continued confidence and trust in me. It is a pleasure knowing and serving you.

To my three sons, I'm sorry I didn't spend much time with you this summer while writing and trying to meet my deadlines. I appreciate you leaving me alone even when you didn't want to. We can play now!

Last but not least, this book is dedicated to my wife Tori. You have encouraged me, supported me, guided me, consoled me, proof-read for me, and were my biggest critic and fan. Thanks for believing in me even when I didn't believe in myself. You've helped me become the man I am today. I love you more than words can express.

Up Close & Personal
with Bill Losey

Birthplace: Yonkers, NY
Hometown: Peekskill, NY

First car: 1987 Toyota Tercel
First job as teenager: Lifeguard
First job after college: Radio announcer

Favorite TV drama: 24
Favorite TV sitcom: Friends
Favorite TV show of all time: Happy Days
Favorite movie: The Shawshank Redemption

Hobbies: Singing, exercising, reading, playing with my three sons

Favorite vacation spot: Outer Banks – North Carolina
Favorite meal: Chicken parmagiana w/angel hair pasta

Person I'd most like to meet (living): Oprah
Person I'd most like to meet (deceased): Johnny Carson

Most humbling moment: The birth of my first son
Most embarrassing moment: It's too embarrassing to tell

Greatest personal achievement: Being married for nearly 20 years
Greatest professional achievement: Running a thriving business from home
Greatest athletic achievement: Hitting 5 consecutive game winning homeruns

One habit I wish I could control: Cracking corny jokes
Boxers or briefs?: See what I mean?

To read Bill's full biography, please see the "About the Author" section at the end of this book or visit ***www.MyRetirementSuccess.com*** *and click on "About Us", then "Meet Bill".*

My Attorney Made Me Include This

Bill's book is meant to provide you with general investment, financial and retirement information. It is not designed to be a definitive investment guide or to take the place of a qualified financial planner or other professional (because that would be just plain crazy).

Given the risks involved in investing, there is absolutely no guarantee that the strategies or methods suggested in this book will ever be profitable. If Bill could guarantee your results, he'd be passing the Grey Poupon to his wife aboard some pimped-out yacht in Tahiti by now.

Here's the bottom-line: Neither the publisher nor the author assume liability of any kind for any losses that may be sustained as a result of applying the methods suggested in this book, and any such liability is hereby expressly disclaimed. Caveat emptor!

Oh, one more thing...the names of certain individuals and some details throughout this book have been changed to protect confidentiality.

PART ONE

What You Need to Know Before You Say Goodbye To Your Paycheck

"Never continue in a job you don't enjoy. If you're happy in what you're doing, you'll like yourself, you'll have inner peace. And if you have that, along with physical health, you will have had more success than you could possibly have imagined."

~ Johnny Carson

You Can Retire Today!

*"You are never too old to set another goal
or to dream a new dream."*
~ C.S. Lewis

Imagine a world free of alarm clocks, bosses, long commutes, office politics and limited vacation time.

Wouldn't it be nice to call the shots, spend more time with your family and friends, doing only those things that you love to do and are passionate about?

Imagine having the time and money to do what you want, when you want, where you want, with whom you want, at the time you want, on your terms?

That's true financial freedom and autonomy, and I invite you to join me and others like you, who crave it badly.

You see, I define retirement as **making work optional.** Regardless of your age or net-worth, it's about discovering your purpose, living with passion, total self-reliance, transformation and creative self-expression.

My view is not that "Life is too short", but rather that

> **RETIREMENT SUCCESS PRINCIPLE**
> Money is just a tool that helps you get what you want!

"Life is too long not to be doing those things that are fun and rewarding", and that the majority of people in our society and culture don't spend enough time examining these issues. I endeavor to help you clarify, simplify and gain control of the big picture of your life.

I firmly believe that if you love what you do, you'll never "work" another day in your life. I know this for a fact because a few years ago I stopped "working" full-time for someone else. Instead, I designed a home-based business I love and began "playing" full-time for myself and the private clients I serve.

If you're like the majority of baby boomers who don't plan to retire in the traditional sense, and instead plan to re-enter the workforce by downshifting into more satisfying and fulfilling careers (even if they're less lucrative), working part-time or starting your own business, why wait? The question I get most is "Can this be done without jeopardizing my retirement plans?" My answer is a big, resounding YES!

Wanna make work optional?

The questions that follow are some of the same questions I ask my private clients to help them discover or rediscover their goals. I know you want to get to the money stuff, but before we talk greenbacks, you need to have clarity and really know what's important to you. Remember, money is just a tool to help you get what you want!

So let's play! Go grab a refreshing drink and get yourself a pen or pencil. Then, take a few minutes to answer these questions. Don't over analyze them; just answer them from your heart (not your head).

1. If money and health were no issue, how would you spend your time?

2. What things in life do you feel are most important right now?

3. What types of activities would you like to participate in that you're not now? Who would you participate with?

4. If you could, what would you be doing differently now?

5. What major life changes do you see in the next 3-5 years?

6. What would you like your ideal future to look like in 5 years? 10 years?

7. What is your greatest hope?

8. What is your greatest concern?

9. What is your greatest passion? (If you're not doing this, what is holding you back? Money, time, confidence, experience, etc.?)

10. What would you attempt to do if you knew you could not fail?

BONUS QUESTIONS

George Kinder has provided the financial planning industry with some critical insights and tools in his valuable book *The Seven Stages of Money Maturity*. Here are 3 questions he offered in his book that I ask my clients to answer that sometimes leave us emotional and in tears. Before you begin, you may want to grab a tissue or two.

Take a few moments to answer these questions. They cut to the core of what you're truly passionate about and reflect your true desires.

1. How would you change your life, now and for the future, if all of a sudden you knew you had "enough" money, whatever that means to you? (Don't be limited by realism. Let yourself dream and expand what you can do, be or experience).

2. You have just learned that you only have 5 years to
   live. Your life will be cut short, without pain and
   without notice. Knowing that death is waiting for
   you sooner than expected, how will you change
   your life? In the uncertain but substantial period
   left to you, what will you do differently with your
   life?

3. You just found out that you only have one day to live - you will die tomorrow. What are your feelings? What longings do you have? What regrets do you feel? What deep and unfulfilled dreams do you have? What do you wish you had attempted or completed, been, had or done in this life that is about to end?

 WARNING! If you've chosen to skip these exercises, you're doing yourself a huge disservice. Please go back! The answers, thoughts and feelings you express here will form the foundation for the rest of your life. As Larry the Cable Guy would say, "Git-R-Done!"

Confessions of a Financial Planner

"The biggest risk is not taking one."
~ Author Unknown

Years ago, when I first got into the financial planning business, I thought it was all about money and numbers. Input this figure, determine how much money someone needs, build a spreadsheet, crunch some numbers, and presto...financial success is guaranteed! Boy was I wrong.

The older I get and the more gray hairs I grow, the more I've realized that what I do has very little to do with money. After 9/11, clients were coming to see me and wanted reassurance that they were going to be okay. I felt like a motivational speaker, pastor and psychologist all at the same time.

The problem is that while I recognized I could provide reassurance, I couldn't guarantee a thing. And that's when it hit me. Everyone, *especially people who are retiring or already retired, wants certainty.* Certainty they'll be okay. Certainty they won't outlive their money. Certainty they'll live happily ever after. But I can't guarantee squat and neither can you. I know it's kind of harsh but it's the truth and the type of straight forward, non-sugar coated advice I provide. And if you remember anything from this book, remember this. In fact, read it out loud with me now.

> **All financial planning and investment decisions are based upon assumptions. Assumptions create expectations. Expectations create guarantees in my mind. But in reality there are no guarantees. The more I resist this fact, the more susceptible I am to disappointment and failure.**

Think about it for a moment....

Do you really know what return you'll earn on your money? No. Your performance could be better or worse than expected.

Do you really know what the inflation rate will be in the future? Nope. Inflation could be more or less than projected.

Do you really know what the tax rates will be? No. Tax laws can and will be changed, and rates could be increased or decreased.

Do you really know if you'll be downsized or let go by your employer? Nope. Your company could eliminate your position with the stroke of a pen or offer you a big fat raise.

Do you really know if we'll get attacked again? No. I hope and pray it doesn't happen but we're dealing with a bunch of whacko's.

Now, say it with me people: "I can't guarantee squat!"

Again: "I can't guarantee squat!"

One more time and a little louder: "I CAN'T GUARANTEE SQUAT!"

That's right. You can't guarantee a thing and neither can I. Good. Now that we're on the same page, let me share with you some of the biggest risks we face. I'll also share with you the unique and humorous way I educate people of these risks and how to overcome them. Let's get to it!

> **RETIREMENT SUCCESS PRINCIPLE**
>
> "I can't guarantee squat!"

THE "OBVIOUS" RISK

In late 2001 and 2002, when the stock markets were heading south in a big way, Mary, a 53-year old widow was really concerned about the value of her portfolio, which was down approximately 10%. I explained to her that when you invest in stocks, volatility and fluctuation are the price you pay for trying to stay ahead of inflation. "But I heard stocks average 10% growth per year", she said.

Listen, dear readers, stocks don't go up in a straight line every year. Will they average 10% per year? Maybe. Maybe not. It's anyone's guess. Will stocks perform better than bonds each year? Probably not. Will they "skyrocket" and "plummet" (media speak)? Sometimes! Hey, I'm no boy scout, but you've got to "Be Prepared".

U.S. Stocks

1997: 33.4%
1998: 28.6%
1999: 21.0%
2000: -9.1%
2001: -11.9%
2002: -22.1%

Source: Ibbotson Associates

Now, say it with me people: "I can't guarantee squat!"

To make my point, I created a book called *101 Stock Market Guarantees* by fictitious authors, Ivana Retyre and her husband, Dr. Ken I. Retyre. Say their names slowly again and you'll see that their names are actually frequent comments and questions I get from prospective clients.

Obviously, there are no guarantees – so here's the kicker. The book contains nothing inside but blank pages. There are no words! After people open the book, fan the pages, and put two and two together, they crack up. It's my lighthearted way of making the serious point that there are no guarantees.

By the way, you can stop smiling now. I mean it...stop smiling. You've got readin' to do. Get serious. This is your money and your life we're talkin' about here.

Listen, this is an "obvious" risk, but for some reason, people think that stocks should ALWAYS go up - every year. It doesn't work that way. Now, does this mean that you should abandon the stock market? Absolutely not! In fact, all of my private clients maintain at least some portion of their money in stocks. It does mean, however, that you need to know what you're invested in and how much risk you're taking with your money. We'll talk more about that in Chapter 4.

Visit **www.101Guarantees.com** *and click on the* **101 Stock Market Guarantees** *button to view and order this book. It makes a great gag gift!*

THE "SILENT" RISK

I call this risk the "silent" risk because it's always there but you never see it. I'm talking about inflation, people.

How do I keep up with inflation?

The stuff you buy today is gonna cost you more tomorrow, and the year after that, and the year after that. And even at a low inflation rate of say 3%, you'd need to double your income in approximately 20 years just to maintain the standard of living you have today.

	1964	1984	2007
Gallon of milk:	$1.06	$1.94	$3.06
Loaf of bread:	$0.21	$0.71	$1.97
A new car:	$2,350	$6,294	23,000
Gallon of gas:	$0.25	$1.27	$3.00
New home:	$30,000	$110,610	$221,000
Average income:	$6,080	$12,866	$34,335
Dow Jones:	874.13	1,211.57	13,000+

Source: Spectrum Unlimited, LLC

In other words, if you're living on 50k today, you'll need 100k twenty years from now. Put another way, if you live on 50k today, it will only buy 25k worth of goods and services twenty years from now.

> **"Stocks are the only asset class to historically outpace inflation over time."**

Do you have an investment strategy in place that is designed to double your income in twenty years? If you don't or you're not sure, I'll tell you how in Chapter 6. And guess what, my suggestions will include that you keep some money invested in stocks that are subjected to the "obvious" risk. Why? Because stocks are the only asset class to historically outpace inflation over time. You need some money there.

THE "EMPLOYEE" RISK

I once heard Joan, a former supervisor, agonizing over having to terminate Bob. She was upset because she knew Bob needed the money, had children to support, and she was going to ruin his life. As it turned out, Bob really didn't like his job, but needed the income and was too scared to make a change himself. Now that the change was made for him, he was able to realize a lifelong dream of starting his own business.

Necessity is the greatest mother of all invention! Let's face it - you are never more creative then when you're in a jam and your back is against the wall. The world opens up to you and you realize all the choices you do have, and can propel yourself toward what you truly want.

Nearly 20 years ago I was laid off twice in four years and had six different jobs! It was during a recession and my prospects for steady employment didn't look good. I was shocked. How could this happen to me? Why me? As it turns out, it was the best thing to ever happen because that's when I made the decision to enter the financial services industry.

Stuff happens and you can't control most of it. Lay-offs

and downsizings happen and you shouldn't be surprised if and when it happens to you. Get real. Your employer doesn't owe you anything. You may think they do, but that's a topic for a whole other book. Your financial well-being is your responsibility. Businesses are in business to make money. Period!

Now, say it with me people: "I can't guarantee squat!"

Listen, expecting job guarantees from your employer is a recipe for disaster. The best example of this would be all of the recent pension plan changes. Employers are closing their plans to new hires, reducing benefits, and freezing benefits for current participants, which means no further pension benefit's will accrue beyond those earned to date. That means you'll need to save more of your own money to fund your lifestyle. Another major issue is expecting that your company will provide lifetime health insurance at no cost. Surprise! You've now got to pay part of your premium!

> **RETIREMENT SUCCESS PRINCIPLE**
> Expect and embrace change.

Things can and do change all the time. Don't get complacent. Don't get lulled into a false sense of security. Go back to school, take continuing education classes, learn or update your skills, and network, network, network. Don't wait for that disaster to happen; do it now. Remember...there are no guarantees!

To make this point, I created another book called *101*

Employment Guarantees by fictitious authors, Owen Kash and Will B. Fired. You know the drill...say their names slowly again and have a good laugh. Since there are no guarantees, this book contains nothing inside but blank pages too. Check out the testimonial by Anita Payczech - it's a hoot!

Visit ***www.101Guarantees.com*** *and click on the* **101 Employment Guarantees** *button to view and order this book. It makes for a hysterical and inexpensive college graduation gift!*

THE "GOOD NEWS/BAD NEWS" RISK

Ron and Margie, 60 year old clients of mine, met with me recently to review their progress and we got talking about his health issues. Like many caring husbands, Ron is concerned about Margie's well-being should he pass away first. While talking with them, I mentioned a story I read about living to age 100 and how that was a goal for me. Ron said, "Bill, I'd like to live to 100 too, but the thought of my 70 year old son moving back in with us scares the hell out of me". We all broke out in hysterical laughter together.

Fact: 7 out of 10 female baby boomers will outlive their husbands and can expect to be widows for 15-20 years. Source: U.S. Administration on Aging

Listen, here's the good news: you're living longer. Now, here's the bad news: you're living longer. That means you'll need money set aside to last for potentially 30 years or longer. This is also called "longevity" risk.

Will you live a long, healthy life and expire peacefully in your sleep? That's what most of us hope for.

Will you be sick or need some sort of assistance as you get older? Possibly.

Will you contract some medical condition that requires around-the-clock care? Maybe.

Will science develop a new medical breakthrough or treatment to cure cancer and other diseases, and prolong our lives for an additional 20 years? That'd be nice.

Now, say it with me people: "I can't guarantee squat!"

Life happens, stuff happens, and you can't control most of it. So like that old television commercial used to say, "Eat right, exercise and take your Geritol® everyday".

Listen, the future is filled with unknowns. This is old news. But this is why planning for retirement is a challenge. Frankly, if we all knew when we'd die, retirement planning would be easy. Unfortunately, since we don't know when our time will be up, we've got to enjoy ourselves today and be active participants in the planning process, going with the flow, and making changes along the way as needed.

To make this point with the people I serve, I created another book called *101 Health & Medical Guarantees* by fictitious authors, Dr. Ben Sewd and Dr. Lyah Bility. Again, since there are no guarantees this book contains nothing inside but blank pages. Be sure to read the testimonial by a lady named Vi Agrah - it's a riot!

Visit ***www.101Guarantees.com*** *and click on the* **101 Health & Medical Guarantees** *button to view and order this book. It makes for a great medical journal or book for patients, nurses, doctors, health care workers and your favorite waiting room.*

THE "RELATIONSHIP" RISK

Post 9/11, I was quite surprised at the number of clients who opened up to me about their marriages and relationships. It was a real eye-opener for me. I mean, I'm a financial planner for Pete's sake, not some marriage counselor (although I've been with my wife Tori for 20+ years). But 9/11 made some clients stop and think: Do I really want to wake up next to this person for the next 2 or 3 decades?

Being comfortable in your relationship is a good thing, but getting too comfortable can spell T-R-O-U-B-L-E or D-I-V-O-R-C-E. When we become too comfortable, we may start to assume that our relationship is secure and we no

longer have to work on it. Being complacent in a relationship can lead to taking it for granted, and may make you
blind to any "issues" and cause you to "check out".

To make my point, I created a book called *101 Marriage
Guarantees* by fictitious authors, Will B. Strong and Faith
Enlove. Say their names slowly again and have a good
laugh. Since there are no guarantees this book contains
nothing inside but blank pages too. And check out the testimonial from Anita deVoors. My female clients roar with
laughter when they see it.

Listen, the bottom-line is: marriages fail and relationships fail. And when they do, it can really mess up your
finances.

So, say it with me people: "I can't guarantee squat!"

My dear readers, when was the last time you sent a card
to your honey bunch? When was the last time you gave a rose to your sweetie pie? When was

> **RETIREMENT SUCCESS PRINCIPLE**
>
> With some thought, creativity, and action, you can keep your relationships and finances in order.

the last time you pinched your significant other on the
behind and gave them a little wink? When was the last
time you did something special for that special someone? If it's been more than a few months, put down this
book right now and go do something nice. These little
gestures could go a long way toward helping you have a

successful retirement. You can thank me later.

*Visit **www.101Guarantees.com** and click on the **101 Marriage Guarantees** button to view and order. This book makes a funny gift for brides, grooms, shower and wedding favors, and bachelor/bachelorette parties.*

THE "UNKNOWN" RISK – STUCK BETWEEN IRAQ & A HARD PLACE

Kathleen, a 57 year old client and divorcee, came to see me in early 2002. She was in tears, fearful and afraid of when we'd be attacked again, and how this would affect her impending retirement. I remember holding her hand and passing her tissues while trying to reassure her we'd get through this. Together, we talked about all things the government was doing to help protect us.

Fast forward 6+ years and we haven't been attacked again yet. There have been dozens of terrorist attacks in other countries, and many plans/attempts have been thwarted both domestically and internationally. Recently, a chilling terrorist attack was stopped in New York as authorities arrested members of a terrorist cell planning to destroy Kennedy Airport. Just a few months ago, the government quietly drafted a doomsday plan that outlines the White House role after terror or natural disaster strikes. The public portion of the new "National Continuity Plan" contains few details and has caused even more anxiety.

I am not a pessimist or a doomsayer, but if you're a realist like me, you know at some point we'll probably be attacked again on U.S. soil. I mean, do you really think the government will be able to thwart ALL potential terrorist threats?

So...say it with me people: "I can't guarantee squat!"

> **RETIREMENT SUCCESS PRINCIPLE**
> Don't assume the government can and will take care of you in an emergency.

Remember Hurricane Katrina & New Orleans? No one cares more about you and your family's safety than you. Have a plan. For example, John, one of my private clients created his own disaster plan. He has a list in a lock box at home that contains instructions and what things he'd want in case he'd have to evacuate, i.e., pictures, computer backups, tax returns, passport, checkbook, credit cards, etc.

Use Katrina as a learning tool. What would you do if your house were destroyed? Where would you go? How would you get there? What if you couldn't leave your home? Develop a plan. Practice your plan. Make sure your family members know their responsibilities.

Expecting the government to take care of your personal security is another recipe for disaster. The assumption that Washington will care for you leads to the expectation you will be cared for. Our complacency is the greatest cause of our future exposure to risks.

To prove my point, I created another blank book, *101 Homeland Security Guarantees*, by fictitious authors, Hugh B. Kairful and Justin Case. Since there are obviously no guarantees, this book contains nothing inside but blank pages as well. It's a light-hearted way to make a serious point. And make sure you check out the testimonials by Al Kyda and Will Findem.

Listen, if we do get attacked again, how will this affect the stock markets, your portfolio, your income and retirement? It's anyone's guess. So, what's your game plan? If you don't have one, I'll talk in greater detail about what's working for my private clients a little later in Chapter 6.

*Visit **www.101Guarantees.com** and click on the **101 Homeland Security Guarantees** button to view and order. This book makes a great journal or inexpensive gift for those in the military, law enforcement or government.*

QUESTIONS & ACTIONS

1. Do you know how much risk you're taking with your investments? ❑ Yes ❑ No

2. Do you have an investment strategy designed to double your income? ❑ Yes ❑ No

3. Are you being complacent with your job or relationship? Do you have your own disaster plan? ❑ Yes ❑ No

4. Do you eat right, exercise and take your Geritol® every day? ❑ Yes ❑ No

5. What's one action you will take today that will change your life for the better?

Retirement Myths vs. Reality

"Truth is so rare that it is delightful to tell it."
~ Emily Dickinson

One of the biggest mistakes people make when planning their retirement, if not **the** biggest mistake, is listening to the wrong people. To this day, it never ceases to amaze me how so many intelligent people take advice from people who are totally unqualified to give it.

For example, when I conduct retirement and investment seminars, it's not uncommon for me to hear statements like this:

"My sister's, ex-husband's, brother-in-law's, former neighbor who used to live next to an accountant said I should do this…"

Or

"I read an article in a financial magazine that says all retirees should do that…"

And so on and so on. You catch my drift?

My dear readers...STOP THE MADNESS!!

Please stop taking generic advice for the masses from those radio/tv/print outlets whose goal is to sell advertising and drive revenues, not build you a secure retirement.

As a bonus, go to **www.myRetirementSuccess.com** and click on the link for a **"FREE 30-Page Report – The 10 Biggest Mistakes People Make When Retiring & How to Avoid Them."** My FREE report will be emailed to you within a few moments.

RETIREMENT SUCCESS PRINCIPLE
Your financial situation is unique and different. Just like no two fingerprints are alike, no two retirements are the same either.

Here are some of the more common myths perpetuated in society by the media and a dose of reality.

RETIREMENT MYTH #1: You'll need 70-80% of your pre-retirement income to live comfortably in retirement.

How much money do I need to retire?

RETIREMENT REALITY CHECK: Are ya kiddin me? Come on people...can a journalist possibly know what's best for you? Has he or she reviewed your finances? Do they know your goals and desired standard of living? Is the article only intended for you? Give me a break! Now that you've got an extra 40-80 hours per week on your hands, do you think you'll spend more money?

The income needed by you to live comfortably in retirement could be a lot more or less. Some of my private clients live on 70-80% of their pre-retirement income. Some live on 90-100%. Some live on 100%+ of their pre-retirement income because they're traveling more, dining out more, completing home renovations, and/or their medical costs have increased. One client, Toni, a 53-year old minimalist, can live on less than $1,000/month. It all depends upon your goals.

Actual Expenses – Post-Retirement

28% - about the same
27% - somewhat higher
25% - somewhat lower
12% - significantly higher
8% - significantly lower

Source: Fidelity Research Institute 2007 Retirement Index

RETIREMENT MYTH #2: You should make your investment portfolio more defensive when you retire.

RETIREMENT REALITY CHECK: Hello....earth to my dear readers. Why should you retire and get more defensive? What does defensive mean anyway? Should you go to 100% cash or 100% bonds? Is that too defensive? Don't you need some stocks in your portfolio or is that too risky in retirement?

If your portfolio was set up correctly from the get-go, why would you have to change just because you stopped

> **RETIREMENT SUCCESS PRINCIPLE**
> How much risk you take with your portfolio is a personal decision.

working? I recently met with a 75 year old man who has had 100% of his money in individual stocks for 40+ years. He understands the risks and is comfortable with that. Conversely, I have two young women in their early 20's as clients. They are new to investing, are trying to get comfortable with the market fluctuation, and only have about 60% of their money in stock mutual funds. This is appropriate for them *at this time*. You see, your situation and attitude will change over time. When it does, you have the option of changing your investment strategy. The old days of "set it and forget it" are over. Retirement <u>may be</u> a time to make a change but it doesn't <u>have</u> to be.

RETIREMENT MYTH #3: Your investment portfolio performance has to beat the S&P 500.

RETIREMENT REALITY CHECK: Why does it have to beat the S&P? Who cares? Listen, benchmarking your returns to a traditional index changes the target away from your goals, to an external measure that you have no control over, and has no real relevance to your goals. So stop worrying over it! For example, I have a 60 year old client, Don, whose goal is to double his investment portfolio in 5 years so he can retire a multi-millionaire. In order for that to happen, he needs to earn 15% per year. We have established an aggressive portfolio over-weighted in international stocks to put Don in the best possible position to achieve this goal. A year later, Don asked if had beaten the S&P 500. He had, but I told him we're not worried about the S&P 500 and what it does. Our investment strategy has nothing to do with it. We're worried about Don and how well Don does. Will he meet his goal consistently? I don't know, but how well the S&P 500 index performs isn't a concern.

Listen, I phased away from us-ing traditional benchmarks such as the S&P 500 and Dow Jones

> **RETIREMENT SUCCESS PRINCIPLE**
>
> Benchmark your progress toward the accomplishment of your goals; not some arbitrary measure.

Industrial Average years ago. Instead, I benchmark my client's progress toward the accomplishment of their life goals. *That is, what return do you require to prevent yourself from running out of money given the lifestyle you desire?* This clearly puts the emphasis on areas we have control over such as:

- reducing risk
- minimizing taxes
- minimizing investment fees
- portfolio rebalancing
- proper beneficiary planning
- and selecting and monitoring proven money managers

You should do the same for yourself!!

RETIREMENT MYTH #4: You can rely on the equity in your home to retire secure.

RETIREMENT REALITY CHECK: Don't bank on it. Sometimes you can. Sometimes you can't. Remember my "I can't guarantee squat!" mantra? Talk with people in Vegas, California and Florida who bought during the recent housing boom at the peak of the market and who are now stuck with big mortgages and negative equity. Real estate doesn't always go up and often times will go down in value.

> **RETIREMENT SUCCESS PRINCIPLE**
>
> **Every** investment and **every** wealth-building strategy comes with its own risks.

Listen, real estate is a great way to build wealth *over time*. The long-term trend is positive. In fact, some of my wealthiest private clients are fortunate to own multiple properties. But if you're basing your retirement success on a short-term "flipping" strategy or "interest-only loans", hoping to see a run up in prices, you may be kidding yourself. Take time now to reevaluate your housing situation. Is it time to refinance, consolidate debts or relocate? In the decade prior to your retirement, try going on a debt diet and redirect those funds to your retirement accounts instead. Remember, every investment and every wealth building strategy comes with its own risks. Like the Chief on the hit TV show *Hill Street Blues* used to say, "Be careful out there".

RETIREMENT MYTH #5: You'll continue working until your late 60's or early 70's.

RETIREMENT REALITY CHECK: Sure it's possible, but 40% of us will be forced out of the workforce due to corporate restructuring, a medical issue, or a family medical issue. I see this all the time. While working into your late 60's is possible and great in theory, it doesn't happen too often. Besides, do you really want to work that long? It's a great planning idea if you love your work or you're short on savings, but if you're like most baby boomers I work with, you're tired and burnt out and want more free time.

RETIREMENT MYTH #6: You don't need to save. You're gonna receive a large inheritance.

RETIREMENT REALITY CHECK: Don't count on it. Years ago, many financial services firms were saying that the biggest transfer of wealth would be passed down to the next generation. Guess what? It hasn't materialized. People are living longer and need the money to survive. Additionally, medical costs are ever-increasing, so there isn't much left over.

RETIREMENT MYTH #7: You can live on Social Security.

RETIREMENT REALITY CHECK: Social Security wasn't meant to be the sole source of your retirement income. If you're lucky, it may provide 1/3 of your desired income in retirement. You'll either need to work longer, reduce your standard of living, or save more.

QUESTIONS & ACTIONS

1. Have you calculated how much money you'll need in retirement? ❑ Yes ❑ No

2. Have you reviewed your portfolio in the last 3 months? ❑ Yes ❑ No

3. Do you have a method for determining if your portfolio is meeting your goals? ❑ Yes ❑ No

4. Are you relying on Social Security or the equity in your home to fund a secure retirement? ❑ Yes ❑ No

5. What's one action you will take today that will change your life for the better?

CHAPTER FOUR

Asset Allocation: More Important Than The Investments You Own?

"Money doesn't make you happy. I now have $50 million, but I was just as happy when I had $48 million."
~ Arnold Schwarzenegger

HOW EMOTIONS AFFECT INVESTING

Tim and Julie, age 60 and 59 respectively, retired at the end of 1999 with their investment portfolio cracking the $1 million mark. They had it made... or so they thought. Every weekday, Tim watched the business channel to see what all the investment gurus had to say.

You see, Tim was a 'long-term, buy and hold investor', and during 2001-2002 he sat tight and watched as his diversified portfolio dropped 15%. After hearing some guru on TV, he panicked and sold his entire portfolio to cash. Tim felt good because his money was "safe" now. But within 7 days, the markets calmed down, the dark clouds were lifting, and within a few months had gained back 8%.

Tim was still nervous, so he watched and waited as the markets rose week after week. The market rebound continued and increased by another 5%. Tim finally felt he was missing out and decided to invest all his money again. **Guess what happened next?** After missing out on the rebound, Tim invested just in time to catch another severe correction, exacerbating his own situation and jeopardizing his and Julie's retirement. Now, his portfolio was down more than 25% from its all-time high.

One of my biggest professional roles is to help my private clients achieve their goals. The way I see it, I have an obligation to help ensure that they not only accomplish their financial goals, but they achieve them with as little stress and worry as possible. So turn off the business channel and stop watching the negative news. Get off the couch and do something fun with your life!

> **RETIREMENT SUCCESS PRINCIPLE**
> You need someone or something to act as a "buffer" between your emotions and investment behavior.

Listen, most of us encounter strong emotions when dealing with money issues. This is understandable. Money has a lot to do with our feelings of success, safety, and self-worth, but it also provides a huge, tangible impact on our lives and the freedoms it provides. The trouble comes when emotions drive your investment behavior. Emotions often spark reactive, short-term decisions that end up being counterproductive to your long-term financial security. In the '90's, it was all about greed. Now, it's all about fear. The world's instability, played out in the media daily, makes people do things they wouldn't normally do because others are doing it or advocating it. The events that we've seen such as 9/11, the military campaigns that followed, and national security issues – all can encourage people to make emotional decisions. In good times and challenging times like these, you need someone or something that can serve as a "buffer" between your emotions and investment behavior.

THE SCIENCE OF SUCCESSFUL INVESTING

What would you say if I told you that the return you earn on your money has little to do with your ability to pick good investments (security selection)?

What would you say if I told you that the return you earn on your money has little to do with knowing when to buy or sell certain investments (market timing)?

What would you say if I told you that the vast majority of the return you earn on your money can be attributed to how well you divide up your money among the major asset classes – stocks, bonds and cash (asset allocation)?

RETIREMENT SUCCESS PRINCIPLE

How soon you retire, your expected rate of return, how much risk you take, how much money you can take out, and how long your money will last, are greatly affected by your asset allocation decision.

When you realize that whether or not you achieve your financial goals will depend, in large part, on how well you position your assets, you'd have to say it's one of

the most important decision's you'll ever make. The
ultimate goal, of course, is a secure retirement. <u>How
soon you retire, your expected rate of return, how much
risk you take, how much money you can take out, and
how long your money will last, are greatly affected by
this one decision.</u> As a result, I spend a tremendous
amount of time on the asset allocation decision with
my private clients.

	Conservative	Moderate	Aggressive
Stocks	30%	50%	75%
Bonds	50%	40%	25%
Cash	20%	10%	0%

This hypothetical asset allocation example is being used for illustrative purposes only.

Unfortunately, many people still believe that trying to
"time" the market and picking the next "hot" investment are the keys to success in reaching their investment
goals. The financial media, and some investment companies, still perpetuate this myth. For example, financial
magazines and rating services consistently publish ever-
changing lists of the "best funds to own now" or "the
5 stocks to buy today" or "the only investment you'll
ever need". Many people turn to these publications for
advice but these lists are backward looking and *cannot*
predict future success. So…say it with me people: "I
can't guarantee squat!"

Listen, to be a successful investor, you need to view investing in the context of risk. **So rather than worrying about picking individual investments, the initial focus of your investment strategy should be on deciding how much you want to hold in stocks versus bonds, domestic versus international, value versus growth, and large-cap versus small cap.** Notice how I didn't mention anything about particular companies or sectors here?

JARGON 101

Stock: ownership of a corporation represented by shares that are a claim on the corporation's earnings and assets.

Bonds: an 'IOU' issued by a government, company or municipality that obligates the issuer to pay the bondholder interest at predetermined intervals, and to repay the principal amount at maturity.

Domestic: U.S. based investments – stocks and bonds.

International: Non-U.S. based investments – stocks and bonds.

Value: investment style where managers look for companies they believe are undervalued, but whose worth will eventually be recognized by the markets.

Growth: investment style where managers look for

companies with above-average earnings growth and profits, which they believe will be even more valuable tomorrow.

Large-cap: the value of a corporation as determined by the market price of its issued and outstanding common stock; i.e., big companies you've heard of such as GE, GM, Microsoft, etc.

Small-cap: the value of a corporation as determined by the market price of its issued and outstanding common stock; i.e., small companies you've probably never heard of but that are still worthy as investment vehicles.

Generally speaking, stocks are more volatile than bonds. Small caps stocks are more volatile than large caps. Growth stocks are more volatile than value. A domestic-only portfolio or an international-only portfolio will be riskier than a diversified portfolio that contains money in both. From year to year, no one, and I mean NO ONE, will be able to predict with any certainty what the best performing asset class will be. So, as a result, you'll probably want to own a little bit of everything.

*It's important for you to see how the best and worst asset classes are constantly shifting and changing. As a bonus, go to **www.MyRetirementSuccess.com.** Click on the "Free Resources" button and select "Article Archives". Then, click on the link that says, "**Asset Class Returns for Key Indices**". This 1 page color chart is simple and easy to understand, and will illustrate how various asset classes have performed over the past 20 years.*

DIVERSIFICATION:
IT AIN'T SEXY, BUT IT WORKS

TV and radio shows, magazines and newspapers have one job. Their job is to get lots of viewers, listeners and readers so they can justify their ever-increasing rates to advertisers. The media loves the hype, the controversy, and the scandals. It gets ratings. They sell the sizzle, not the steak. Just look at their headlines about the stock markets "Skyrocketing" and "Plummeting". They pay copywriters big bucks to come up with catchy headlines that intend to evoke an emotion in you so you'll watch, listen and buy their subscriptions. Let me tell you, don't buy the sizzle - you need the steak! We're all looking for that silver bullet or magic pill to make everything better. Well, here it is – DIVERSIFICATION.

Diversification is a strategy that seeks to reduce investment risk while maintaining a desired rate of return by spreading your money out over a number of different types of investments. It takes advantage of the tendency of different asset types to move in different cycles and thus smooth out the ups and downs of your portfolio.

> **RETIREMENT SUCCESS PRINCIPLE**
> Diversification seeks to reduce volatility in a portfolio but it can neither guarantee superior returns nor guarantee against losses.

My diversification process normally begins with an analysis of the historical levels of risk and return for each asset type (stocks, bonds, cash) and sub-styles (large-cap, small cap, growth, value, domestic, international) being considered. These historical values are then used as a guide to structure a portfolio that matches your goals and overall level of risk tolerance.

Have your eyes glazed over yet?

*To see how different allocations have performed historically over the past 80 years, go to **www.MyRetirementSuccess. com.** Click on the "Free Resources" button and select "Article Archives". Then, click the link for "**Asset Allocation Risk and Reward**". This simple 1 page chart will explain things easily in a visual manner.*

BALANCING RISK & REWARD

So what's the right asset allocation for you? Before I answer, let me explain something. Prior to developing and presenting recommendations to a new client, I usually have a few meetings with them to understand their needs, goals, and concerns. And yes, we go through the same questions you answered in Chapter 1 plus dozens of others. What can I say, I'm thorough.

I'll have clients complete a 25 question and a 5 question risk tolerance questionnaire. These questionnaires were designed by a behavioral finance firm that has integrated investment research with investor behavior into a unique profiling tool. Next, I'll review all of their financial statements to see where they're at compared to where they want to be, and I'll score their two risk profile questionnaires.

Then, and only then, do I come back with a *customized* asset allocation recommendation. I'll explain the various options, expected range of returns, expected risk, the pros and cons, features and benefits, etc. Total time required to accomplish all this stuff – approximately 8 - 12 hours.

Now, I don't say this to impress you, but instead to impress upon you that the **asset allocation decision** is one of the most serious pieces of the retirement planning puzzle. In case you missed it earlier, <u>how soon you retire, your expected rate of return, how much risk you take, how much money you can take out, and how long your money will last, are greatly affected by this one decision</u>. But you don't have an extra 8 - 12 hours to read a big fat book now and I don't have the room to share all that information here. Like you, I've got people to see and things to do. But I can't leave you hangin' either, so let me show you a sample portfolio, or two or three.

SAMPLE PORTFOLIOS

The sample portfolios that follow may be appropriate for my private clients but they may not be right for you. These are over-simplified allocations to make it easy to understand. You should only use them as a starting point for a discussion with your spouse, significant other or a qualified advisor.

(a) Target Allocation	(b) Expected Range of Returns - EROR	(c) 1 Year Expected Risk Range
40% Stocks/60% Bonds	5%-9%	-10%
60% Stocks/40% Bonds	6%-10%	-15%
80% Stocks/20% Bonds	7%-11%	-25%

a. These scientifically balanced portfolios are built using low-cost index funds, enhanced index funds, and ETFs (exchange traded funds). The sample allocation models each contain approximately 8 - 12 investments so we can have broad diversification across varying asset classes such as large cap growth, large cap value, mid/small cap growth, mid/small cap value, international equity, emerging market equity, emerging market debt, government bonds, high yield bonds, international fixed income, and REITs. Allocation models are automatically rebalanced when the actual allocation deviates from the target allocation by 3 - 5%. This helps us employ the buy-low, sell-high discipline.

b. Expected Range of Returns cannot be guaranteed and are shown net of all transaction costs, investment expenses and investment management fees (assuming a maximum annual cost of 2%). This is your projected bottom-line over long periods of time.

c. 1 Year Expected Risk Range cannot be guaranteed and assumes the worst expected percentage decline in any 12 month period. During the prolonged 2000-2002 bear market, a diversified 60/40 model declined by approximately 20% over those 3 years combined, but recouped the entire loss and more over the next 15 months.

So the bottom line is you need to discover how much risk you're comfortable with so you can make the all important asset allocation decision.

*As a bonus, go to **www.MyRetirementSuccess.com**. On the homepage, locate the section labeled "Have You Lost Confidence In The Investment Advice You're Getting?" and click the link: "Learn A Better Way to Invest". This area of my website will illustrate 5 important principles that should form the foundation of your investment portfolio.*

QUESTIONS & ACTIONS

1. Do you make investments or changes to your portfolio based upon emotions? ❑ Yes ❑ No

2. Do you know what your asset allocation is?
❑ Yes ❑ No

3. Is your portfolio broadly diversified among varying asset classes? ❑ Yes ❑ No

4. Do you systematically rebalance your portfolio to maintain your desired level of risk? ❑ Yes ❑ No

5. What's one action you will take today that will change your life for the better?

What Wall Street Doesn't Want You To Know

"The real measure of your wealth is how much you'd be worth if you lost all your money."

~ Author Unknown

I conduct dozens of free teleseminars, public seminars and adult education workshops throughout the year at area high schools, colleges and credit unions. One of the most highly attended is a retirement investing workshop I present with the same name as this chapter, *What Wall Street Doesn't Want You To Know.*

I usually begin my presentation by flashing a slide from the projector screen on the wall. It contains industry jargon like this: Value. Growth. Blend. Equity. Fixed-income. Large-cap. Small-cap. Mid-cap. Indexes. Corporates. Government bonds. Treasuries. Separate accounts. Short-term bonds. Long-term bonds. International. Global. Emerging markets. Stocks. Bonds. Muni's. REITs. ETFs. Spiders. Vipers. Commodities. Sector funds. Private equity. Hedge funds.

I read through each type of investment or asset class and say, "As you may already know, putting together an investment portfolio is hardly user-friendly. So tonight

I'm gonna talk about how you can build an investment portfolio you can <u>understand</u> and how you <u>pay</u> for it."

That's what we'll accomplish together in this chapter.

THE HIGH-PROFILE & LOW-PROFILE MARKETS

Colgate. Disney. IBM. Pfizer. Ford. 3M. GM. GE. Microsoft. These are just a few examples of companies that comprise what I refer to as the high-profile market. We hear about these companies and read about them. We see their advertising and TV commercials, and we use their products and services all the time. How many of these companies do you recognize? If you're like most people who attend my seminars and you have a pulse, you recognize most or all of these companies.

Now, let's look at some other U.S. companies...

Ocular Sciences. Sunrise Senior Living. Black Box Network Services. Monaco Coach. Bob Evans. Midway. Kilroy Realty Corporation.

How many of these companies do you recognize? If you're like most people who attend my seminars, you may recognize one or two, and in some instances three. But I've never had anyone say they recognize four or more of these companies. These are all substantial, successful companies, so how is it you're not familiar with them? They're part of what I refer to as the low-profile market. Let's compare the two side by side. I'll be using some industry jargon here but I'll try to keep it simple and easy to understand.

High-Profile Market	Low-Profile Market
Large companies	Small Companies
Well-known	Less well-known
Widely owned	Narrowly held

The high-profile market is made up of very large "blue-chip" companies and is often referred to as large-cap stocks (or large capitalization). The name "large-cap" reflects the huge total value of a companies stock. For example, anywhere from roughly $10 billion to $300 billion dollars (in the case of General Electric and Microsoft).

On the other side of the ledger, the low-profile market is made up of relatively smaller companies often referred to as "small-cap" and "mid-cap". Low-profile companies are considerably less well-known, while high-profile companies are very well known. High-profile stocks are widely owned by many investors like you and me, while low-profile stocks are less likely to be owned by the average investor.

Simple enough, right?

HOW THEY PERFORM

Now, let's compare how they perform as investments. To do this I've looked back over the past 80 years and lumped together all of the companies that were historically part of the high-profile market. On average, an investment in these stocks grew about 10.4% per year. So if you've ever heard that "stocks average 10% per year", this is probably what journalists and the mass media are referring to.

What about the low-profile market? How did this perform? Well, over the same time frame, the stocks of smaller companies performed even better at 12.7% per year.

Now, at this point in my seminar or workshops, hands start to go up and a common question I hear is: "Why not just invest in smaller companies?"

> **RETIREMENT SUCCESS PRINCIPLE**
> Past performance doesn't guarantee future results.

Well, there's a very good reason NOT to. First of all, there are never any guarantees that investment history will repeat itself. And yes, I know it's been a while, so say it with me people, "I can't guarantee squat!"

Even more important, you need to recognize that while the low-profile market has given investors a better return than the high-profile market over time, the "ride" isn't the same. In fact, large-cap and small-cap stocks have very different rides. Sure, the value of the high-profile, large-cap stocks fluctuates up and down, but the low-profile, small-cap stocks typically have a rougher ride over shorter periods of time. The bottom line is that stocks of small companies tend to rise and fall in value more dramatically from day-to-day, and month-to-month. And this up and down volatility can be quite upsetting when it's your retirement money we're talking about.

But despite the extra volatility of small cap stocks, there is a very good reason to invest in both small caps and large caps, and it has to do with wealth building. At first glance, it might seem that there's not much of a difference between 10.4% and 12.7%, but over time this 2.3% differential could literally mean the difference between retirement success and failure. In fact, a 2% performance difference could literally mean an investment portfolio with tens of thousands or hundreds of thousands of extra dollars to spend over your lifetime. It's significant!

So what do you do? Invest in both, but not the same way. More on that in a moment.

MARKET EFFICIENCY & COSTS MATTER

I believe the high-profile, large-cap stock market has proven to be a very hard market to beat over time. So in this area, it makes more sense to join the market rather than try to beat it. And there are two basic reasons for it: market efficiency and costs.

Let me explain market efficiency in terms of the high-profile market. Large-cap stocks, basically the 200-300 largest companies in the country, are continually picked over and studied by Wall Street analysts, the financial and news media, and by millions of investors. And that's why financial gurus say the high-profile market is an "efficient market". An efficient market is one in which all of the relevant information on each company's stock is readily and widely available, and the information has already been factored into the stocks price. So in this kind of market, it's virtually impossible for anyone, even professional analysts and investment managers, to gain an edge in picking which stocks will rise and produce a bigger reward for investors.

Now, earlier I mentioned costs. We know it's hard for large-cap managers to outperform other large-cap managers because they're all acting on the same information. And when you factor in management fees and transaction costs, most managers can't even meet the benchmark. You see, each investment or mutual fund has its own internal cost structure, called an expense ratio. This is a direct cost to you which is buried in the prospectus in small print with all the other legalese that most investors never read.

Here's the arithmetic on large-cap mutual fund expenses. The fees the manager charges each year for managing the fund averages around 1.5% of all the dollars in the fund. Transaction costs which include the costs of buying and selling securities in the fund are estimated to average about nine-tenths of a percent. This gives the fund manager a 2.4% handicap to make up before he or she even gets started.

LARGE-CAP FUND EXPENSES

Fund Management Fees = 1.5%

+ Transaction Costs = 0.9%

Handicap = 2.4%

So, for example, if a large-cap index earns 10% for the year, a large-cap fund manager has to earn 12.4% just to break even with the market. Let me take a moment and re-cap.

Because of market efficiency and costs, I'm a staunch advocate of using low-cost index funds, enhanced index funds and/or exchange traded funds (ETFs) as investment vehicles in the large-cap portion of your portfolio. An index fund has many advantages but let me name just a few. First, an index fund or ETF will enable you to own a broadly diversified basket of stocks. And because the goal for the manager is to replicate a benchmark and they are not being asked to analyze or actively manage these stocks, this allows management fees and transaction costs to be kept to a minimum. Their goal is simply to buy and hold a particular basket of stocks.

Now, let's get back to the low-profile market. Remember how I said earlier there are reasons to invest here as well? One big reason is because of its performance over the long-term. But it's a lot more volatile too. And while every large company started out as a small company, not every small company becomes a large one. So, in this area, it takes expertise, diligence and time to find companies that will survive, grow and flourish. The hard part is that there are over 9,000 small and medium size companies that make up the low-profile market. Given the size of these companies and their multitude, it's only natural that each of them receives much less attention. As a result, fewer people know about them, fewer analysts cover each company and fewer investors are likely to own them. These are the hallmarks of an "inefficient market". An inefficient market is a market in which all of the relevant information on each stock is NOT readily and widely available. So here, professionals have the potential to beat a benchmark through hard work and intelligence.

So that's why I say you invest in both high-profile and small-profile stocks differently. You probably can't beat the efficient high-profile market consistently, so you join it by owning an index fund, enhanced index fund or ETF to get a broadly diversified portfolio at a low cost. And, in the inefficient, low-profile market, where a talented portfolio manager has the potential to beat a benchmark, you should consider investing in an actively managed fund or managed account. And to help you understand this simply and easily in a way you should be able to comprehend, I offer my clients the opportunity to use something called a **Skill-Weighted Portfolio**™.

THE SKILL-WEIGHTED PORTFOLIO™

There's a raging debate within my industry as to the best way to invest. In fact, a few years ago I attended a financial planning continuing education conference in Florida, where portfolio managers of actively managed funds debated with portfolio managers of passively managed investments (index funds and ETFs) for nearly 3 hours.

> **What's the best way to invest?**

These gentlemen expressed their individual philosophies and there were many passionate moments as each defended the merits of his/her opinions. There were a lot of points made, opinions expressed and biases evident. And depending on who was talking, it would be hard for anyone to argue with them because they both made valid points. They put on quite a show.

After the presentation, I went and spoke with each portfolio manager privately and after probing them to death, they each admitted that their philosophy didn't work in every type of market or in every type of asset class all the time. This is what Wall Street doesn't want you to know!!!!

So what is the best way to invest? Should you only invest in low-cost index funds? Should you invest in actively managed funds? Should you invest in a combination of investments?

At the next break-out session I had the pleasure of being introduced to the **Skill-Weighted**™ method of investing. And, for the first time, investing was made simple, not only for me as a professional, but in a way my clients could understand.

The **Skill-Weighted**™ method of investing is based on three clear, sensible premises:

KEY PREMISES

Premise #1: Market Efficiency Matters – because how much value active portfolio management can add to your bottom-line primarily depends on market efficiency. (And as I've already pointed out, markets like large-cap stocks derive little or no value from active management).

Premise #2: Costs Matter – so the fees you pay for investment management should be and can be correlated to the managerial value you actually receive.

Premise #3: Realistic Expectations Matter – because when you know what to expect over the short-term, you tend to be more comfortable and are able to remain invested longer. (And as I've already

> pointed out, having someone or something to serve as a buffer between your emotions and investing behavior is critical to your success. Don't be like Tim in Chapter 4!)

If you base your investing on these three premises, it can lead to the potential for enhanced performance. But here's the problem...most people are not following these premises. Most people have no idea what they're actually invested in. Most people have no idea what their asset allocation is. Most people don't know how much risk they're subjecting themselves to. And most have no idea how much money they're paying in dollars and cents for their investments, and if they're receiving value for what they're paying.

Hey, if you're a busy baby boomer, you probably have many different investment accounts and types of funds and investments at various financial institutions. It isn't uncommon for me to meet with a prospective client who has 5 - 15 different accounts with a whole cornucopia of investments. Don't worry, you're not alone.

"How you structure your portfolio can be every bit as important as what you put in the portfolio."

Most investors use a conventional portfolio structure that is typically represented by a colorful pie-chart (that looks like a multi-colored pizza) showing all the specific types of assets they own.

But I dig a little deeper and want you to dig a little deeper too, because I believe that <u>how you structure your portfolio</u> can be every bit as important as what you put in the portfolio. So I want you to change from this conventional portfolio structure to a simpler three-tier structure of a **Skill-Weighted Portfolio**™. The three tiers are called...

- The Efficient Market Core (or, the "EM Core" for short)
- The Active Ring
- The Alpha Rim

((**Skill·Weighted**Portfolio
3-Tier Structure

Based on the name of the EM Core, you've probably figured out already that this structure is based upon market efficiency.

- The EM Core holds investments in the efficient, high-profile market (such as large-cap stocks and investment grade bonds)

- The Active Ring holds investments in the less efficient, low-profile market (such as small-cap stocks and high yield bonds)

- The Alpha Rim is reserved for certain types of special opportunities (for example, people are hearing more and more about investment opportunities in far-off countries like China and India, and may want to invest in a mutual fund or ETF that focuses on one of these countries, or a particular sector such as natural resources, technology or utilities).

((Skill·Weighted Portfolio

Management Matched to Market Efficiency

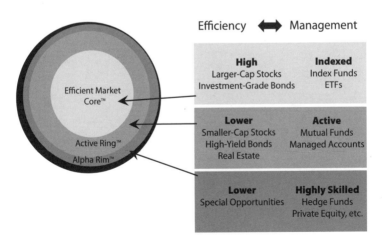

Based on the First Premise which tells us that managerial value depends on market efficiency, you can build your investment portfolio with the same three tiers and the appropriate type of management.

- In the EM Core, indexed investments are the most appropriate. They allow you to inexpensively "join the market" rather than pointlessly trying to "beat it". For you golfers out there, EM Core is "Par" with the market which is very, very good. These indexed investments are available in a few forms I spoke about earlier; index funds, enhanced index funds, and exchange traded funds.

- The Active Ring, which holds investments in the inefficient, low-profile market, is appropriate for "active" managers who use their skill and experience to try to outperform a particular benchmark. Here, actively managed investments and/or enhanced index funds are typically owned in the form of managed accounts or mutual funds.

- The Alpha Rim, which is for special opportunities, utilizes managers who have highly specialized skills to exploit highly specialized opportunities. And, although I'm not a market-timer, I believe there are times when a manager can exploit market "misbehavior" due to greed and fear.

((Skill'Weighted Portfolio

Management Matched to Market Efficiency

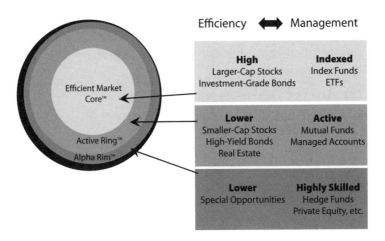

Efficiency ⬌ Management

Efficient Market Core™

Active Ring™

Alpha Rim™

High	Indexed
Larger-Cap Stocks	Index Funds
Investment-Grade Bonds	ETFs

Lower	Active
Smaller-Cap Stocks	Mutual Funds
High-Yield Bonds	Managed Accounts
Real Estate	

Lower	Highly Skilled
Special Opportunities	Hedge Funds
	Private Equity, etc.

When you match the type of management to market efficiency in this way, the managerial fees (your investment costs) in each of the three tiers become correlated to the manager's potential to add value just as the second premise says it should.

- In the EM Core, the index funds, enhanced index funds and ETFs are essentially unmanaged so the fees (expense ratios) are appropriately very low.

- In the Active Ring where managers (of mutual funds and managed accounts) have the potential to add value, moderate fees should be expected.

- The Alpha Rim, managers are expected to add a high degree of value and the fees here will generally be higher. However, you can keep your costs low here by using indexes and ETFs as well.

((Skill•Weighted)Portfolio
<u>Fees Correlated</u> to Value-Added

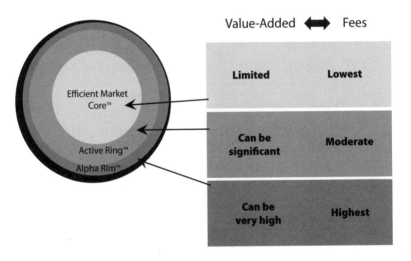

This 3 Tier Structure offers another big advantage as it conveys clearer, more realistic performance expectations:

- In the indexed EM Core, essentially the same performance as the broadly held stock market (and the bond market, if you have bonds in the Core).

- In the actively managed Active Ring, your goal is long-term performance that's "above market", although you should also expect the potential for greater volatility over shorter periods of time.

- The Alpha Rim, you would expect long-term returns that are significantly better and somewhat independent of the overall market.

((Skill·Weighted Portfolio
Clearer, More Realistic Expectations

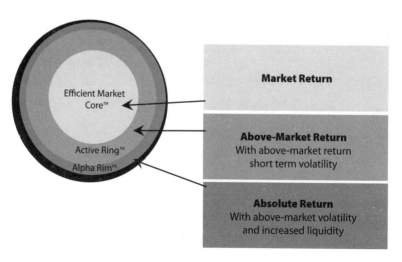

So, if you know what to expect over the short-term and the long-term, you may just be a more patient investor which is one of the keys to successful investing (and something I can write a whole other book on at another time).

Let me sum it up for you with this chart:

EM CORE	ACTIVE RING	APLHA RIM
Efficient Markets	Inefficient Markets	Inefficient Markets
High-profile	Low-profile	Special opportunities
Large-cap	Small/Mid-Cap	International/Sector
Inv. Grade Bonds	High Yield Bonds	Emerging Markets
Index funds/ETFs	Actively Mgd. Funds	Actively Mgd. Funds
Enhanced Index Funds	Managed Accounts	Exchange Traded Funds
Join the market	Attempt to beat market	Attempt to beat market
Low fees	Moderate fees	Higher fees

To listen to a free recording of my teleseminar, "What Wall Street Doesn't Want You To Know", go to **www.MyRetirementSuccess.com.** *Click on the "Free Resources" button and select "Audio Programs". Then, click the link in the first paragraph. A complimentary transcript of the audio program is also available for download on the same page.*

QUESTIONS & ACTIONS

1. Do you know what you're invested in? ❑ Yes ❑ No

2. Do you know how much your investments are costing you? ❑ Yes ❑ No

3. Have you read the prospectuses for your investments? ❑ Yes ❑ No

4. Are you getting good service and value for what you're paying? ❑ Yes ❑ No

5. What's one action you will take today that will change your life for the better?

Creating Income for Life

"I've got all the money I'll ever need,
if I die by four o'clock"
~ Henny Youngman

When your paycheck stops, what's the best way to create a predictable, sustainable and increasing stream of income that will last? Where should you start? What direction do you take? Is there an efficient way, a strategic way, to tap your savings and investments, and take money out to live on? Is there a way you can spend interest-only and never touch your principal? As you contemplate these questions, know that there are tons of ways and countless ideas and investment products/programs designed to do just this. I'll tell you what you need to consider, as well as what to watch for and avoid.

HOW MUCH DO YOU NEED?

The very first thing you need to do is figure out what kind of lifestyle you want. Will you be traveling more? Doing renovations? Relocating to a more or less expensive area? Chillin' out with your friends and family? Eating out every night? Starting your own business?

WHATCHA GONNA DO? You need to figure this out so you won't be bored.

Next, you need to assess how much money this lifestyle is going to cost you. Will your expenses be more than, less than or about the same as when you were working and generating an income? Have you accumulated money in various accounts that will be enough to generate a sufficient income so that you can live the life you envision? Hopefully, the choices you've made in the past have prepared you for this moment.

My/our estimated monthly expenses are: _₱6000._

WHAT ARE YOUR SOURCES OF INCOME?

If you're one of the fortunate few who has a monthly pension, congratulations! Not many people have them any more and they'll become even less of a factor for future generations.

Are you eligible now and taking Social Security? Will you be working and have any earned income? How much dough will you have rollin' in every month?

My/our monthly pension is/will be: _____

My/our monthly Social Security is/will be: _₱700._

My/our monthly earned income
from work is/will be: _____.00_____

My/our monthly anticipated income from all "other"
sources is/will be: _____6204._____

My/our monthly total projected
income is/will be: _____$700._____

DO THE MATH!

My total monthly projected income _____$700._____
MINUS my estimated monthly expenses _$6000.____
leaves me with _____-$300.____ each month.

<u>Do you have money left over OR are you coming up short?</u>

HOW MUCH HAVE YOU SAVED?

If you're like most people I come across, you'll need to tap your savings and investments to supplement your other income sources. That's what the money is there for, isn't it? You've done a good job at saving and accumulating a six-figure or seven-figure portfolio. You've probably saved for decades in employer sponsored retirement plans like a 401k or 403b, or through self-directed plans like IRA's, Roth IRA's and annuities. You may have also been fortunate enough to have the cash-flow to save additional monies in non-retirement accounts such as a joint account with a spouse or significant other. Way to go! Now, let's spend some of it.

The amount you have accumulated and the type of account it's in can play a part in the "timing" of where you'll take and receive income from. Depending on your tax bracket, in many cases (but not all)

> **RETIREMENT SUCCESS PRINCIPLE**
>
> In many cases (but not all) it's usually better to take money out of non-retirement accounts first.

it is usually better to take money out of non-retirement accounts first for more favorable tax purposes. This allows for your tax-deferred monies to continue to grow and compound without the effects of taxation today. Please consult with your tax preparer or a qualified advisor to decide what is best for your situation.

The total amount of money I/we have in
<u>retirement</u> accounts is: _$228,000._

The total amount of money I/we have in
<u>non-retirement</u> accounts is: _$216,000._

The grand total of money I/we have is: _$444,000._

HOW TO CREATE "PREDICTABLE" INCOME

Creating a steady stream of predictable income is easy. It's as simple as picking up the phone and talking with your current investment provider. Tell them you'd like to begin receiving money on a regular, recurring basis. For example, some of my clients like to take money two times per month to replicate their former biweekly paychecks. Others prefer money once per month. Some take money quarterly, semi-annually or annually. A few just take it on an as-needed basis. Regardless, most investment companies (mutual fund companies), and to a lesser extent insurance companies and banks, offer great flexibility when it comes to getting your hands on your money. Each company has its own policies and procedures, and it's highly likely that you'll have to sign distribution forms and paperwork to make it happen. Finally, you should have the flexibility to have your provider issue you a physical check or transfer the funds electronically. I suggest the latter because you'll have less paperwork, you'll save time, and know funds are available on a certain day each month without having to worry about it.

You can instruct your investment provider to pay you the dividends and interest your investments earn each month. Under this arrangement, the amount of money you receive will fluctuate slightly from month to month but you will not be touching your principal. Other people opt to have their investment provider send them the same amount of money every month. This is typically known as a systematic withdrawal, where you will receive the same dollar amount of money on whatever pre-determined frequency you establish. In this latter example though, it's possible that you could be liquidating a portion of your principal if the amount of money you take out is greater than all the interest, dividends, and capital growth combined.

> "The less money you take out, the lower inflation is, the lower your investment costs, and the higher the rate of return you earn on your money, the longer your nest egg will last."

HOW TO CREATE "SUSTAINABLE" INCOME

Creating a sustainable income stream is harder since we don't know how long we're gonna live. With a healthy diet, regular exercise, good times with family and friends, anything is possible. Will your retirement last 10 years, 20 years, 30 years or 40+ years? It's anyone's guess. That's why it is so vitally important to monitor how much you'll take out of your accounts (as a percentage of your overall portfolio) at least once per year. Obviously, the less money you take out, the lower inflation is, the lower your investment costs, and the higher the rate of return you earn on your money, the longer your nest egg will last. Conversely, the more money you take out, the higher inflation is, the higher your investment costs, and the lower the rate of return you earn on your money, the shorter your nest egg will last.

How much money can I take out?

Most people in my industry believe that withdrawing 4% of your nest egg per year beginning in year one and then increasing the amount of the withdrawal every year to account for inflation is a prudent strategy. Unfortunately, this 4% rule has become gospel in my industry because of some number crunching and analysis using historical data. But what if history doesn't repeat itself? What if we run into a prolonged period of negative or low investment returns (bear market)? What if we have a prolonged bull market (markets go up)? What if you want more than 4%? Listen, the future cannot be predicted with any certainty. There is no magic number. It varies from person to person. I have some private clients who take out much more than 4% and some who take out less. Consequently, I'll comment on how I address this issue later in this chapter under **The "Safe-Money" Benchmark Strategy™** section.

How much money you need for retirement depends a great deal on how long you expect to live. As a bonus, go to **www.MyRetirementSuccess.com.** *Click on "Free Resources" and then click "Calculators". Scroll through the "Index" on the right side and locate the "Life Expectancy Calculator". It will give you an idea of your life expectancy based upon your current age, smoking habits, gender (sorry guys, we're going before the ladies), and several other important lifestyle choices.*

> **Author's note:** I plan on being around until I'm at least 100 but that darn thing said I'm checking out at 82.5. I guess I'd better enjoy these next 40 years.

HOW TO CREATE "INCREASING" INCOME

Creating increasing income is vital to your retirement success because the cost of goods and services is always going up. I mentioned this earlier but even at a low inflation rate of 3%, you'd need to double your income in approximately 20 years just to maintain the standard of living you have today. That is why it is so important for individuals to maintain at least a portion of their money in the equity (stock) markets.

> **RETIREMENT SUCCESS PRINCIPLE**
> You should keep at least 40% of your money invested in stocks.

In fact, I normally recommend that my private clients, regardless of their age, keep at least 40% of their money there. I know past performance is no guarantee of future results, but as of now, the equity markets have been the only asset class that has consistently delivered returns above inflation over long periods of time.

INCOME-PRODUCING INVESTMENT VEHICLES

Growing longevity and a low interest rate environment

are a huge problem. As a result, boomers like you and me really need to think and strategize how we'll finance a 20 - 40 year retirement. Here are a few alternatives to consider that may be appropriate for your investment portfolio.

How much money will my investments generate?

Bonds: They add instant diversification and risk reduction to a stock portfolio, and generate recurring income. When you buy a bond, you're actually lending money to a government, a municipality, a government agency or a corporation. In essence, the bonds they issue are a short-term or long-term IOU's. Bonds can be purchased individually or through a bond mutual fund. Bonds are subject to interest rate risk.

Income Mutual Funds: They normally invest in a variety of dividend-paying stocks, corporate bonds, government bonds or a combination of these, depending on the funds objectives. Mutual funds are subject to market risk and may be worth more or less when you sell them.

Dividend-Paying Stocks: Some companies, like GE, distribute part of their profits to stockholders in the form of a dividend. If profits increase, the dividend can be increased. If profits decrease, the dividend can be reduced. This is a great vehicle to get potential growth on your assets and income as well.

Reverse Mortgages: These have become more popular in recent years as retirees are sitting on homes with a lot of equity build-up (but none of my clients have used them as of yet). A reverse mortgage can convert the equity in your home to an income stream. Cash received can be paid to you in one fell swoop; as a regular recurring monthly payment; as a credit line that let's you decide when and how much you want paid out; or as a combination of any of these methods.

This is just a quick sampling of some investment vehicles that are popular with retirees. They may be or may not be right for you but they're a good starting point to research and discuss with your spouse, significant other or advisor.

ANNUITIES:
THE GOOD, THE BAD & THE UGLY

Another type of retirement income investment vehicle that's getting a lot of press nowadays is the tax-deferred annuity. And, I gotta tell you, in my nearly 20 years of advising people about their finances, no topic confuses or polarizes retirees more than annuities. People either love them or hate them. Very few of my clients actually own them but annuities can and do play an important part in some retirees lives (like my mom and dad).

> "Annuities can and do play an important part in some retiree's lives."

There are literally hundreds of different contract types and thousands of options to choose from. Often times, the media portrays insurance companies as the bad guys and writes scathing articles about bad annuity contracts, bad salesman, questionable sales tactics and high fees. Sometimes these journalists make valid points, but many times I find they really do retirees a disservice with negative, one-sided articles. Personally, I'm not emotionally attached to annuities or any product, so I'll try to be fair and balanced like that cable news channel, and let you decide.

Are annuities a good investment?

So, let's start at the beginning. An annuity is a contract between you and an insurance company. Your money grows tax-deferred inside an annuity until you take it out. It is an insurance-based contract designed specifically to protect you against the possibility of living too long and outliving your assets. If you're afraid of outliving your money, you may very well be happy to invest some portion of your portfolio in an annuity as they are the only vehicle that will guarantee you an income stream for life. I'll talk more

> **RETIREMENT SUCCESS PRINCIPLE**
> Annuities are the only investment that can guarantee you an income for life. Guarantees are subject to the claims paying ability of the insurer.

about those "guarantees" later but for now let's get you acquainted with annuities and the various types.

PARTIES IN AN ANNUITY CONTRACT

1. **The insurance company:** the entity that issues the annuity contract.

2. **The annuity owner:** the person who contributes money to the annuity contract.

3. **The annuitant:** the individual whose life is used to determine the payments.

4. **The beneficiary:** the person or entity that receives annuity proceeds and payments on the death of the annuitant or the policy owner.

TYPES OF ANNUITY CONTRACTS

1. **Immediate Annuities:** You give money in a single, lump sum to an insurance company and in return they guarantee to pay you a regular income stream for a certain period of years or for life. The older you are, the more money you invest, and the shorter the payout period, the more money the insurance company pays you. Payouts begin immediately.

2. **Deferred Annuities:** You give money to an insurance company in a lump sum or in multiple deposits and your money will grow tax deferred for a period of time. At a future point, you can have funds paid out to you, generally through monthly payments over

a specified period of time, or your lifetime or the joint lives of a couple. Payouts are deferred.

TYPES OF DEFERRED ANNUITIES

1. **Fixed Annuities:** A type of annuity contract offering investors a minimum interest rate guaranteed by the issuing insurance company. The rate can and will be adjusted up or down. Fixed annuities are useful for risk-averse investors seeking a stable, predictable return. Interest rates are generally slightly higher than a bank CD.

2. **Variable Annuities:** A type of annuity contract where the buyer has the option of investing in mutual-fund-like investment options called sub-accounts where returns are not guaranteed. Within these sub-accounts, you can choose from many investment options such as stocks, bonds, balanced, domestic, international, precious metals, money markets, etc. The available choices vary from contract to contract and your variable annuity contract value will move up and down with normal stock and bond market fluctuation. This type of annuity allows you to invest to provide future benefits that will keep pace with or surpass inflation.

3. **Equity-Index Annuities or Fixed Index Annuities:** A type of fixed-rate annuity that combines a guaranteed minimum interest rate (i.e., 3%) with the potential for greater growth. Returns are normally based on a complex formula tied to a specific market index such as the NASDAQ or S&P 500. If your selected

index rises during your contract period, a higher rate of return (above the guaranteed minimum interest rate) will be credited to your annuity contract for that period. Unlike a variable annuity, if the markets decline, typically the worst you can do is to earn the contracts guaranteed minimum interest rate. This type of annuity allows you to pursue market gains while protecting your principal.

INCOME OPTIONS

Now that you understand the types of deferred annuities, let's review the various ways you can take money out of one.

1. **Lump-sum withdrawals:** You can take out all of the money in your contract in a single lump sum. When you do this, the annuity contract is considered surrendered and it no longer exists. Depending on the type of annuity and how long you've had it, the insurance company may impose a surrender charge. A CDSC or contingent deferred sales charge is a penalty the insurer will assess, usually expressed as a percentage of your balance, if you don't hold it for a certain minimum length of time.

2. **Partial withdrawal:** Most annuity contracts have a built in stipulation that you can withdraw a certain portion of your entire account value each year (usually 10%), without incurring a sales charge.

3. **Lifetime Annuities:** You can receive the highest monthly payment with a life only annuity that's good for as long as the annuitant lives. However, when that person dies, payments stop, even if the policy owner has received less than what was initially invested. This is called annuitization or annuitizing your contract.

4. **Lifetime Annuities with Terms Certain:** You will receive regular payments for the life of the annuitant or for a specified number of years, whichever is longer. If the annuitant dies before the term of years has passed, the beneficiary will receive annuity payments for the remainder of the term.

5. **Term Certain or Period Certain:** You will receive regular payments for a pre-selected number of years (5, 10, 15, 20, 25, 30). The longer the desired payout period, the lower the payment you will receive. If the annuitant dies before the specified period has been reached, payments continue to the named beneficiary for the balance of the term.

6. **Joint and Survivor:** This is when two individuals will receive regular payments over their two lives. When one person dies the annuity payment or a specified portion of the annuity payment will continue to the survivor for his/her lifetime.

7. **Refund Options:** Regular payments are received over the life of the annuitant. But if the annuitant dies before the policy owners investment has been fully recovered,

the balance is refunded to a beneficiary. Refund options are a feature you can pay the insurance company more for to include in your contract.

LIVING BENEFITS

After the bear market of 2000-2002, insurance companies began offering living benefit options in their variable annuity contracts. These guarantees help protect your nest egg from the ups and downs of the stock market but come at an additional annual cost. Living benefits can add .25% to 1.10% in annual fees to the typical .75% to 2% in annual costs of a variable annuity. Nonetheless, these living benefits are worthy of your consideration.

> **Will I outlive my money or will my money outlive me?**

1. **Guaranteed Minimum Income Benefits (GMIB):** This benefit provides assurance of a certain level of income in the future.

2. **Guaranteed Minimum Withdrawal Benefits (GMWB):** This benefit provides assurance that you can withdraw a certain percentage of your investments annually, in some cases for life.

3. **Guaranteed Accumulation Benefits (GAB):** This benefit provides that after a set number of years, usually 10, your account will be worth a minimum level, even if your investments decline in value.

4. **Guaranteed Lifetime Withdrawal Benefits (GLWB):** This benefit provides a payout guaranteed for life. Additionally, the owner may surrender her contract at any time and receive the net value of the account.

ANNUITY GUARANTEES

As you can see, I've used the word "guarantee" frequently throughout the past few pages. You should know that that word, when part of an annuity contract, typically has an asterisk (*) attached to it. The disclaimer that goes along with "guarantee*" normally says something like this: "Guarantees are subject to the claims paying ability of the insurer."

I always have fun with this part of my retirement and investing workshops because the question I get often is: "If the "guarantees" are subject to the claims paying ability of the insurance company, does that mean they're really not guaranteed if something goes wrong?" About this time, I pull out my *101 Stock Market Guarantees* book by fictitious authors Ivana Retyre and Dr. Ken I. Retyre. I remind everyone that "I can't guarantee squat!" and we all have a nice chuckle.

Listen, because we all plan on living long lives, this presents a huge risk as well as a huge opportunity for insurance companies. "Longevity" risk or an unexpected and prolonged bear market could potentially put undo financial strain on an insurance company. Certainly insurance companies employ very smart, analytical, number-crunching employees who can figure out how to hedge against stock market and interest-rate moves. But to my knowledge there is no financial hedge against longevity that exists...yet.

In the different industry trade magazines I subscribe to there is a debate going on. Some people are fearful that insurance companies offering "guarantees" are assuming too much risk and are over-extended. Insurance companies respond saying they have complex actuarial models used to monitor risk daily and company official's routinely express confidence in how they manage risk.

> **RETIREMENT SUCCESS PRINCIPLE**
> Understand what you're investing in before you invest in it.

So who is right? Who will win the debate? Only time will tell.

Because of the complexity of many annuity contracts, if you're considering purchasing one, you should consider all aspects, including the tax ramifications, before entering into a contract. Therefore, I strongly suggest you seek the advice and counsel of appropriate and _objective_ tax, legal and financial advisors. Get a second opinion before signing any contracts!

As with any investment, please understand what you're getting into before you get into it. An annuity may or may not be right for your situation. Annuities are not an 'all or nothing' investment vehicle. You can reduce your risk by investing a lesser sum of money among multiple insurance carriers. As an alternative, you may decide to limit your investment in an annuity to a small portion of your overall portfolio.

EXAMPLE

a. Instead of investing $100,000 with one insurance company, consider investing $50,000 with two companies or $25,000 with four companies.

b. If your total portfolio is $500,000, consider limiting your stake in an annuity to 20% of your total portfolio ($100,000).

Be sure to ask your advisor or annuity salesperson about other common annuity provisions such as: bailout provisions, surrender charges, annuity-driven contracts, owner-driven contracts, guaranteed death benefits, enhanced death benefits, exchange privileges, contract charges and fees, and his/her compensation/commission structure and how that affects the contingent deferred sales charge. **Ask them to quantify the fees for you in dollars and cents, and compare that to other investment alternatives.** Do your homework!

The bottom-line: If you're contemplating investing in an annuity contract, you'll want to make sure you're dealing with an insurer who is financially solid. There are credit rating companies such as Moody's, Standard and Poor's, and A.M. Best that provide objective commentary and analysis of an insurer's financial stability and wherewithal.

> **Author's note:** Personally, I've found that if you broadly diversify your holdings (See Chapter 4 on Asset Allocation), and you have realistic withdrawal expectations, you won't need to pay an insurance company for these living benefits. I've also found that a diversified investment portfolios performance often times exceeds whatever minimum protections the insurance company guarantees provide. Furthermore, I've found that when I quantify the actual cost of the living benefits in dollars and cents (not a percentage of assets), most people don't choose to invest in an annuity.

THE "SAFE-MONEY" BENCHMARK STRATEGY™

In this chapter we've covered a lot of ground. I've talked about income producing investment vehicles and products. We've talked about things you should watch out for and avoid. So it's only natural now for you to be wondering what the best way is to create a predictable, sustainable and increasing stream of income from your investment portfolio. Am I right?

It's been my experience that most financial books and advisors talk about money in percentages. However, virtually everyone I talk to talks about money in dollar terms. So let's talk dollars. Every one of us has a number in our brain that we're stuck on. This is a financial benchmark you're trying to accumulate and grow your portfolio to. Your number might be $1,000,000. It could be $250,000. It might be $100,000, $500,000, $2,500,000 or higher. We all have a different number and that's okay!

Interestingly, when people finally hit their self-imposed number, one of two things usually happens. First, either they want to set a new, higher benchmark and grow their portfolio even further (now motivated by greed). Or two, they get nervous because after all the years of hard work and discipline, they don't want to lose it all (now motivated by fear). So, in my practice, I have developed what I refer to as **The "Safe-Money" Benchmark Strategy**™. It's a simple, yet powerful concept, but I've found that my clients sleep much better at night knowing this safe-money income strategy has been implemented on their behalf. Here's how it works.

A few years before retiring, if possible, you should begin to accumulate an amount of money that's equivalent to 1-5 years worth of cash withdrawals (based upon your expected income needs). This systematic accumulation of cash is done on purpose so that you have a safe-money source to pull from when the balance of your investment portfolio and the stock and bond markets may be declining in value. Some people want one year of cash on hand. Some want two years of cash on hand. Some people want three, four or five year's worth of cash on hand. Again, everyone's number is different and that's okay. It all depends on your comfort level.

Each time your portfolio exceeds a pre-established benchmark, you should systematically harvest the excess money above the benchmark, and put it in cash or short-term bonds (money market funds, CDs, and/or U.S. Treasury bills). For example, Sue and John have accumulated $250,000 in their **Skill-Weighted Portfolio**™. Together, we have established $260,000 as their benchmark. Any time the value of their account reaches or exceeds $260,000, we liquidate at least $10,000 and put the proceeds in a money market fund earning approximately 5% interest (as of this writing). This is the money they spend. We build up a cash cushion so when they want to take money out, it comes from an asset class (cash) that isn't subject to market fluctuation.

> **RETIREMENT SUCCESS PRINCIPLE**
>
> Consider accumulating an amount in cash that's equivalent to 1-5 years worth of income withdrawals.

Here's another example: Kay has accumulated $700,000 in her IRA account. We have established $725,000 as her benchmark. Any time the value of her account reaches or exceeds $725,000, we liquidate at least $25,000 and put the proceeds in a money market fund. Kay now has a cash cushion equivalent to four years worth of withdrawals on hand. When Kay's portfolio performance is positive, we liquidate (sell high) and build up more cash to spend.

When Kay's portfolio performance is flat or negative, we simply take withdrawals from her cash cushion. This protects her from having to liquidate shares of her stocks and bonds when they may be declining in value due to normal market fluctuation or a correction.

Here's one more example: Mike and Linda have accumulated $500,000 in their accounts. They live fine on their pensions and social security but want to take some money out to splurge on a big trip once per year. They have established $515,000 as their benchmark. Any time the value of their portfolio reaches or exceeds $515,000, we liquidate at least $15,000 and put the proceeds in a money market fund for them to spend. Mike and Linda have accumulated enough money in cash by using **The "Safe-Money" Benchmark Strategy**™ that they now take longer trips each year and sometimes they even take guests with them!

The "Safe-Money" Benchmark Strategy™ is a total return concept that takes into account your goals, tolerance for risk, and both the growth potential and income potential (interest, dividends and capital gains distributions) of each asset you own. This strategy allows for an inflation-adjusted income stream for you, and greater flexibility when taking money out. Consequently, if managed properly, you should be able to take out more than the standard 4% rule allows for.

The "Safe-Money" Benchmark Strategy™ is best implemented 2 - 5 years before retirement and needs to

be monitored at least annually after retiring. Additionally, the strategy is easier to implement in a retirement
account such as an IRA because there are no tax ramifications until money is actually withdrawn. Individual's
who wish to employ **The "Safe-Money" Benchmark
Strategy**™ in a taxable, non-retirement account, should
consult with a qualified advisor such as an accountant to
learn the most tax-efficient way to harvest these gains.

One final note: once you've accumulated your desired
pot of cash to take money from (1, 2, 3, 4, or 5 years),
consider raising your benchmark to a new higher threshold. For example, since Kay now has four years worth
of cash on hand, we have increased her benchmark from
$725,000 to $750,000. Cash is king but we don't want
too much cash either. You've got to find a balance that
works for you.

QUESTIONS & ACTIONS

1. Do you have a plan to create a predictable, sustainable and increasing stream of income? ❑ Yes ☒ No

2. Do you understand what you're investing in? ☒ Yes ❑ No

3. Have you assembled a team of trusted advisors to help you manage your income in retirement? ❑ Yes ☒ No

4. Does **The "Safe-Money" Benchmark Strategy**™ resonate with you? ☒ Yes ❑ No

5. What's one action you will take today that will change your life for the better?

The
Social Security Dilemma

"Good decisions come from experience,
and experience comes from bad decisions."
~ Author Unknown

"Should I take Social Security at 62 or should I take it later?" This is one of the most common questions I get. So what should you do? It depends on many factors.

Some people should take Social Security at 62. Some people should take it at 63. Some people should take it at 64. And some should take it at their normal retirement age (NRA) which is the age at which 100% of your Social Security retirement benefits are available (with no reduction). Each person's situation is different and you'll want to weigh the pros and cons of taking it early versus waiting. So, let's explore.

> **"Each person's situation is different and you'll want to weigh the pros and cons of taking it early versus waiting."**

SOCIAL SECURITY 101

For those born in 1937 or earlier, your normal retirement age (NRA) is age 65. This is also called full retirement age (FRA). For those born after 1937, FRA/NRA is gradually increased until it reaches age 67 for people like me born in 1960 or later.

If you're willing to accept a permanently reduced benefit, your monthly payout could begin as early as age 62. For example, if your NRA is age 65, collecting Social Security at 62 will reduce your monthly payout by approximately 20%. If your NRA is age 67, collecting Social Security benefits at 62 will reduce your monthly payout by approximately 30%.

> **There is no financial benefit of waiting to take Social Security after age 70.**

In essence, if you choose to take Social Security before your NRA, your monthly benefit is reduced to reflect the fact that this income will now be paid over a longer period of time. Similarly, if you choose to postpone taking Social Security for a few years, your monthly benefit will be increased each year you wait beyond your NRA up to age 70. For example, if you were born in 1943 or later, your monthly benefit will increase by 8% for each year you delay receiving benefits past your NRA up to age 70.

Retirement Benefit as a Percentage of the Primary Insurance Amount at Various Ages[2]									
Year of Birth	Normal Retirement Age (NRA)	Credit for each year of delayed retirement after NRA (Percent)	Benefit as a % of PIA at Age						
			62	63	64	65	66	67	70
1924	65	3	80	86⅔	93⅓	100	103	106	115
1925-1926	65	3½	80	86⅔	93⅓	100	103 1/2	107	117 1/2
1927-1928	65	4	80	86⅔	93⅓	100	104	108	120
1929-1930	65	4½	80	86⅔	93⅓	100	104 1/2	109	122 1/2
1931-1932	65	5	80	86⅔	93 1/3	100	105	110	125
1933-1934	65	5½	80	86 2/3	93 1/3	100	105 1/2	111	127 1/2
1935-1936	65	6	80	86 2/3	93 1/3	100	106	112	130
1937	65	6½	80	86 2.3	93 1/3	100	106 1/2	113	132 1/2
1938	65, 2 mos	6½	79 1/6	85 5/9	92 2/9	98 8/9	105 5/12	111 11/12	131 5/12
1939	65, 4 mos	7	78 1/3	84 4/9	91 1/9	97 7/9	104 2/3	111 2/3	132 2/3
1940	65, 6 mos	7	77 1/2	83 1/3	90	96 2/3	103 1/2	110 1/2	131 1/2
1941	65, 8 mos	7½	76 2/3	82 2/9	88 8/9	95 5/9	102 1/2	110	132 1/2
1942	65, 10 mos	7½	75 5/6	81 1/9	87 7/9	94 4/9	101 1/4	108 1/4	131 1/4
1943-1954	66	8	75	80	86 2/3	93 1/3	100	108	132
1955	66, 2 mos	8	74 1/6	79 1/6	85 5/9	92 2/9	98 8/9	106 2/3	130 2/3
1956	66, 4 mos	8	73 1/3	78 1/3	84 4/9	91 1/9	97 7/9	105 1/3	129 1/3
1957	66, 6 mos	8	72 1/2	77 1/2	83 1/3	90	96 2/3	104	128
1958	66, 8 mos	8	71 2/3	76 2/3	82 2/9	88 8/9	95 5/9	102 2/3	126 2/3
1959	66, 10 mos	8	70 5/6	75 5/6	81 1/9	87 7/9	94 4/9	101 1/3	125 1/3
1960 and later	67	8	70	75	80	86⅔	93 1/3	100	124

Source: Social Security Administration

HOW MUCH CAN YOU EXPECT?

Social Security benefits are based upon your 35 highest earning years. You could potentially receive as much as $24,000 per year in benefits at age 65, but this assumes you've earned a paycheck for at least 35 years. In reality, many retirees will receive less. That's because many people will take Social Security as soon as they're eligible at 62 and get a permanently reduced benefit. Additionally, some people take it at 62 because they have no choice – they've lost their job or can't find work due to an injury or medical condition. Women, in particular, have been known to get much less of a Social Security benefit because often times they tend to have fewer years in the work force due to caring for kids and parents.

MY FAVORITE SOCIAL SECURITY JOKE

Two men were talking. "So, how's your sex life?"

"Oh, nothing special. I'm having Social Security sex."

"Social Security sex?"

"Yeah, you know; I get a little every month, but it's not enough to live on."

Each year the Social Security Administration sends out an annual statement to each worker age 25 and older who doesn't yet receive monthly benefits. When you get yours, you should verify the accuracy of the recorded earnings versus your tax return. The annual statement is mailed approximately one month before your birthday each year. If you'd like to see your report you can request one at www.ssa.gov or by contacting the Social Security Administration directly at 1-800-772-1213.

	Avg. Monthly Benefit Age 62	Avg. Monthly Benefit Age 65	Avg. Monthly Benefit Age 70
2008	$1,228	$1,536	$2,054
2009	$1,259	$1,575	$2,015
2010	$1,291	$1,614	$2,158
2011	$1,323	$1,655	$2,212
2012	$1,356	$1,696	$2,267

Note: Assumes 2.5% annual increase in monthly benefits. Maximum wage earner.

MY #!*&@ SOCIAL SECURITY BENEFITS CAN BE REDUCED & TAXED?

Surprise, Surprise! Your Social Security benefits could be reduced and/or subject to income taxes. You'll need to check with your accountant or tax preparer on that one.

If you are still working and you begin taking Social Security benefits early (before your NRA), your payout will be temporarily reduced if your wages exceed certain limits. For example, if your current age is less than your NRA, $1 of benefits is lost for every $2 you earn over $12,960*. In the year you reach your NRA, $1 of benefits is lost for every $3 you earn over $34,440*. The good news is, once your reach your NRA, there is absolutely no reduction in your monthly Social Security benefits regardless of how much money you make.

RETIREMENT SUCCESS PRINCIPLE
Don't make the Social Security decision in a vacuum. Consult with your advisor and/or a qualified tax advisor.

In general, if ½ of your Social Security income plus your modified adjusted gross income (which is often the same as your adjusted gross income – AGI), exceeds certain limits, then a portion of your Social Security benefits could be taxable. For example, married couples filing jointly with income exceeding $32,000 could have 85% of their Social Security taxed. For singles and all others, there's usually a $25,000 threshold.

*These are 2007 values. This exempt amount is subject to inflation adjustments every year.

WHEN SHOULD I TAKE IT?

This is one of the most important decisions you need to make for a few reasons. First, the decision is irrevocable. Once you make it, you can't change your mind. Second, the initial amount of money you begin receiving from Social Security acts as a base amount from which all future increases will be calculated over your lifetime. Consequently, I'm a big believer in trying to convince my private clients to separate the decision of what age they wish to retire - from what age they want to begin receiving their monthly Social Security benefits. The bottom-line is that these two events don't have to happen at the same time!

If you're mathematically inclined, one way to answer this all-important question is to do a break-even analysis at the Social Security Administration website. The analysis will estimate the age when the total value of your higher monthly projected benefits (from delaying the receipt of a monthly Social Security check to age 63 or later) will be greater than the total value of a lower monthly benefit (from receipt of a monthly Social Security beginning at 62). You can access the break-even analysis tool at the following website: http://www.ssa.gov/OACT/quickcalc/when2retire.html

From my experience, people in poor health or with a short life expectancy may benefit from taking their benefits beginning at age 62, regardless of what the break-even analysis says. Additionally, if you need the cash now, by all means take it. Conversely, if you don't need the money now, you're in good health, you're still working, and have a history of longevity in your family, you should at least consider postponing receipt of your monthly benefits a few years or to your NRA to have a permanently higher amount in the future. In short, if you think you'll live at least until age 77, consider starting your Social Security benefits after age 62. If you think you won't live to age 77, consider taking benefits at age 62 or age 63.

SOCIAL SECURITY MAXIMIZATION STRATEGIES FOR COUPLES

Here's something to consider if you're married. Spouses, especially younger ones and/or ones whose earnings were modest or negligible during their lifetime, may benefit financially by encouraging an older spouse or one with higher earnings to wait until age 70 to collect benefits. That's because a spouse's benefit (usually the wife), is based upon her husbands earnings record when her own monthly Social Security benefit would not equal or exceed 50% of her husbands. Delaying his receipt of Social Security to age 70 could mean a substantially higher monthly income for the balance of her lifetime. And since Social Security could be her only source of inflation-protected income, the decision when to take Social Security shouldn't be taken lightly. Contact the Social Security Administration for particular details about your own situation by calling 1-800-772-1213.

MESSAGE FOR 20-SOMETHINGS, 30-SOMETHINGS, AND 40-SOMETHINGS

Let's face it. The Social Security Trust Fund is in trouble. Increased longevity and the number of people eligible for monthly benefits will grow exponentially over the next two decades. Investment, pension, government, actuaries, public watch-dog groups and concerned citizens have been begging for changes to bolster the long-term viability of Social Security. It is a national debate that always seems to heat up at election time, but than fades away. Hopefully sooner rather than later, Washington will address and remedy this issue once and for all. Whatever changes occur however, you can bet that people in their 20's – 40's will either end up receiving less benefits, have to wait longer to collect them, or pay more into the system to receive them, or possibly a combination of any of these scenarios.

Social Security will not disappear from our national landscape because that would be political suicide for any elected official. But it will be altered in such a way that it will look very different than it is today. Take your financial responsibility into your own hands. Start saving more money for your retirement today! You're gonna need it.

QUESTIONS & ACTIONS

1. Do you know your normal retirement age (NRA)?
☒ Yes ☐ No

2. Do you have a current annual statement from the Social Security Administration illustrating your projected benefits? Have you verified your earnings?
☒ Yes ☐ No

3. Have you consulted with an advisor or your tax professional to learn how taking Social Security could affect your tax situation? ☐ Yes ☒ No

4. If you're married, have you performed a break-even analysis and/or considered delaying receipt of your monthly payout to potentially benefit your spouse?
☐ Yes ☒ No

5. What's one action you will take today that will change your life for the better?

CYA-
Cover Your ASSets

*"The only way to keep your health is to eat what
you don't want, drink what you don't like,
and do what you'd rather not."*
~Mark Twain

Like you, I don't particularly like discussing the possibility of death, disability and destruction. However, if you're successful, have assets to protect, and a family or other people who depend on you, you need to deal with these issues. Doing so now will get it off your 'to-do' list and allow you to enjoy your retirement and life that much more because you won't be wasting energy thinking and worrying about this stuff any longer.

I'm not going to bore you with long passages about the types of life, auto, disability, health, homeowners, liability, and business insurance available. Instead, I'm just going to strongly encourage you to talk with your agent or advisor, and suggest you review your existing policies. What types of coverage do you have? How much are your deductibles? Can coverage be reduced or eliminated? How can you free up money for your retirement while still protecting yourself?

Additionally, I'm going to strongly encourage you to

contact an attorney who specializes in estate planning so you can finally get your ducks in a row and have peace of mind knowing that your loved ones will be cared for and protected. Make sure you talk with your attorney about wills, trusts, health care proxies, medical directives, powers of attorney, etc. Those documents you had drawn up years ago when your first child was born are probably long outdated. It's time to get current. Again, I'm not going bore you with long passages about all the estate planning options available. There's just too many! That's an estate planning attorney's job anyway. Ask them what makes sense for you and develop and/or update your estate plan today!

TO LTC OR NOT TO LTC?
THAT IS THE QUESTION

What I've found is that people, especially retirees, hang on to old insurance policies they no longer need because they're reluctant to change. In doing so, they needlessly pay premiums that cut into their retirement spending, and often times they short-change themselves on coverage they really do need.....like long-term care (LTC) insurance.

Odds of Financial Catastrophes

Catastrophe	Odds
Loss of home	1,200:1
Auto accident	240:1
Medical claim over age 65	40:1
Any LTC episode over age 65	2:1
LTC episode lasting 1-3 years	6:1
LTC episode lasting 3+ years	13:1

Source: Steve Nussbaum Long-Term Care Planning & Insurance

"Transferring some or part of the risk to an insurance company is the least expensive option."

Unlike many insurance agents who will attempt to scare you into buying a long-term care insurance policy, I'm going to assume you're discerning, astute, have done your homework and want long-term care coverage already. You recognize that:

- You'll probably live many more decades
- You'll probably have a medical issue during your lifetime that will require care
- The future cost of medical care is going to be significantly higher than it is today
- Spending down your assets and becoming a ward of your state Medicaid program is not a smart or viable option

- Rolling the dice and potentially paying for care out-of-pocket could jeopardize your retirement security
- Transferring some or part of the risk to an insurance company is the least expensive option

	LTC COSTS (today)	LTC COSTS (projected - 20 years)
Nursing homes	$72,000-$96,000/yr	$190,000-$250,000/yr
Care in your home	$30,000-120,000/yr	$80,000-$320,000/yr
Adult Day Care Centers	$90-$200/day	$240-$465/day
Assisted Living Facilities	$36,000-78,000/yr	$96,000-$206,000/yr

IS LONG-TERM CARE INSURANCE RIGHT FOR YOU?

According to the National Association of Insurance Commissioners, you should **NOT** buy long-term care insurance if:

- You can't afford the premiums (duh)
- You have limited assets
- Your only source of income is a Social Security benefit or Supplemental Security Income (SSI)
- You often have trouble paying for utilities, food, medicine, or other important needs
- You are on Medicaid

According to the National Association of Insurance Commissioners, you **SHOULD CONSIDER** buying long-term care insurance if:

- You have significant assets and/or income

- You want to protect some of your assets and income
- You can pay premiums, including possible premium increases, without financial difficulty
- You want to stay independent of the support of others
- You want to have the flexibility of choosing care in the setting you prefer or will be most comfortable in

Here are the top three reasons why some, not all, of my private clients purchase long-term care insurance:

- They want to protect a healthy spouse from experiencing a loss of financial security and/or a decrease in the standard of living
- They want to protect their family members from having to act as caregivers (and potentially jeopardizing their own financial security)
- They want to maintain their financial independence, dignity and their decision-making authority

MONEY FOR SALE

When you invest in a LTC policy you are protecting your family members from the potential physical, emotional and financial toll a health issue can have on them. This is a significant benefit. But the real value of a long-term care policy is the inflation-adjusted financial benefit it can provide at some point in the future. For example, let's assume Marilyn, age 55, purchases a LTC policy today. The current cost of care in her area is $200/day.

Marilyn invests in a policy with a 5-year benefit period
(1,825 days) that includes 5% compounded inflation
protection. Marilyn's annual premium is $2,500 but her
initial benefit pool is worth $365,000.

- LTC Benefit Pool: $200/day x 1,825 days = $365,000

Now, let's assume Marilyn doesn't require some sort
of care until she's 80 years old. At 5% compounded inflation, the value of her inflation-adjusted benefit pool
would be worth more than one million dollars. In fact,
for $2,500/year in premiums, her policy would provide
a benefit equivalent to $1,236,020! That really puts the
amount of your premium into context. It's actually very
inexpensive given the potential payout. But it gets even
more attractive when you realize that certain policies allow you to deduct all or part of the premium you pay
on your taxes. This makes LTC insurance an even better
deal. Check with your accountant or tax preparer on the
specifics of your situation.

> **"The real value of a long-term care policy is the
> inflation-adjusted financial benefit it can provide at
> some point in the future."**

THE 1% SOLUTION

For most people, the issue isn't whether you need long-
term care insurance; the issue is how to pay for it. As I
said earlier, it's highly likely you are paying for insurance

coverage that you no longer need. Perhaps the kids are grown and the mortgage is paid for, and you no longer need that old life insurance policy anymore. Maybe you can increase a deductible or reduce/eliminate certain coverage to free up dollars that can be used for a long-term care premium. Maybe you can change your investments around to a **Skill-Weighted Portfolio**™ (see Chapter 5) and invest in low cost index funds and/or exchange trades funds (ETFs). This alone could reduce your investment costs and/or enhance your investment returns providing additional cash flow for things like long term care. You can invest in this coverage without having to come up with additional monies out of pocket. Get creative!

One strategy I employ with my clients is what I refer to as the *1% Solution*. Very simply, are you willing to invest 1% of your investments/savings each year to protect the other 99%? For example, if you have $500,000 in investments are you willing to invest $5,000 (1%) to protect the other $495,000? If you have $800,000, are you willing to invest $8,000 to protect the remaining $792,000? This makes a lot of sense.

The reality is most people can get the policy they want with the benefits they want at a cost of usually less than

> **RETIREMENT SUCCESS PRINCIPLE**
> Consider investing up to 1% of your portfolio in a LTC policy each year to protect the other 99% of your assets!

1% of their total investments. In fact, some of my private

clients have invested as little as one-quarter to one-half of 1% of their assets and purchased LTC coverage that is appropriate for them.

Factors that affect policy pricing include:

- the amount of your daily benefit – the lower your daily benefit, the lower the annual premium
- the elimination (waiting) period – the longer your waiting period, the lower your premium
- your age – the younger you are, the lower your premium
- your health status – the healthier you are, the lower your premium
- your benefit period – the shorter the benefit period, the lower your premium

Talk with an independent advisor/agent and have her run you multiple illustrations so you can see the variation in annual premiums by adjusting the daily benefit, elimination period, and the benefit period upward and downward.

BUT WHAT IF I NEVER USE MY LTC POLICY?

I'm sorry but this is the most ridiculous question I am asked. If you never use your LTC policy, consider yourself lucky and fortunate. You've had good health! This is what we should all hope for.

For some reason, people fear paying a LTC premium for a policy they may never collect on. Let me ask you...do you ask this question about your health insurance? Do you ask this question about your auto insurance? Do you ask this question about your homeowners insurance? Or do you want to be ill, have your house destroyed and your car totaled?

Listen, a long term care episode can happen to anyone at any age. In fact, approximately 40% of all LTC episodes are for people under age 65. It's important to remember that LTC doesn't mean nursing home care; it could mean care in your home. Additionally, a long-term care episode isn't always permanent; you may just need care temporarily as the result of an accident, fall, back injury, or car accident.

If you never use your LTC policy...CONGRATULATIONS! I hope you never do!

But remember, stuff happens. So say it with me people: "I can't guarantee squat!" That's why you need to seriously consider LTC insurance! Please don't be penny-wise and pound-foolish!

---

*As a bonus, you can listen to a free recording of my teleseminar, "Long-Term Care Planning 101". Go to **www.MyRetirementSuccess.com**. Click on the "Free Resources" button and select "Audio Programs". Then, click the link in the second paragraph. A complimentary transcript of the audio program is also available for download on the same page.*

QUESTIONS & ACTIONS

1. Can you eliminate or reduce existing insurance coverage to free up cash flow for retirement? ☒ Yes ☐ No

2. Have you met with a qualified attorney and updated your estate planning documents? ☒ Yes ☐ No

3. Is long-term care insurance right for you? ☒ Yes ☐ No

4. Have you met with an independent advisor who can objectively counsel you on the LTC programs available in your state? ☒ Yes ☐ No

5. What's one action you will take today that will change your life for the better?

PART TWO

The Non-Retirement Retirement

"Passion is energy.
Feel the power that comes from focusing on what excites you".
~Oprah Winfrey

Happiness Is A Currency More Valuable Than Money

"The only thing money gives you is the freedom of not worrying about money."
~Johnny Carson

I'm a firm believer that your life should be about playing and fun. The activities you participate in, including your work, should provide satisfaction and fulfillment. More importantly, the work and activities you participate in should be things you're passionate about and things that energize you!

Ask yourself this very important question: "If money wasn't an issue, would I continue doing what I'm doing?" If you answer "YES", then you love what you do and you're playing. Congratulations! However, if you answer "NO", then you should start exploring other options and figure out what you love to do.

WHAT FLOATS YOUR BOAT?

Here's a brief checklist to get you started and help you figure out (or remind you of) some activities that energize you. Take a moment and circle those activities you love to do or wish to try. If you can earn an income doing/teaching these activities, even better! The goal is to pinpoint any activity that brings you fulfillment and substantial satisfaction, and seems like play (not work).

Acting/Drama	Antiquing	Archery
Attending auctions	Attending concerts	Auto racing
Auto repairing	Backgammon	Backpacking
Badminton	Baseball/Softball	Basketball
Bicycling	Billiards/Pool	Bingo
Bird Watching	Bookbinding	Book reviews
Bowling	Boxing	Bus tours
Camping	Canoeing	Card games
Carpentry	Casino/gambling	Ceramics/pottery
Checkers	Chess	Civic Organizations
Coffee Club	Collecting coins	Conservation/Ecol.
Cooking/Baking	Crafts	Cribbage
Croquet	Crossword puzzles	Dancing: Ballet
Dancing: Social	Darkroom work	Designing clothes
Dining out	Discussion groups	Dominoes
Drawing	Driving	Electronics
Embroidery	Encounter groups	Exercising
Fencing	Fishing	Flying/Gliding
Folk Dancing	Football	Fraternal Org.
Gardening	Go to comm. ctrs.	Go to horse races
Go to nightclubs	Go to opera/ballet	Go to plays/lectures
Golf	Gymnastics	Hiking/Walking
Horseback Riding	Horseshoes	Hunting
Ice Skating	Jewelry making	Jigsaw puzzles
Jogging	Judo/Karate	Kite flying
Knitting/Crochet	Leatherworking	Listen to radio
Marksmanship	Mechanics	Metalwork
Miniature golf	Model building	Monopoly
Motorboating	Motorcycling	Mtn. Climbing
Needlework	Painting/Drawing	Parties

Pets/Animals
Playing music instrument
Religious organizations
Rug hooking
Sculpture
Swimming
Singing
Social drinking
Sunbathing
Talking books
Traveling abroad
Volunteering
Watching sports team
Weight lifting
Woodworking

Picnics
Political activities
Roller skating
Sailing
Sewing
Shuffleboard
Skiing
Square dancing
Table games
Talking on phone
Visiting friends
Volleyball
Watching TV
Window-shopping

Playing Poker
Reading
Rowing/boating
Scrabble
Shopping
Sightseeing
Skin Diving
Squash/handball
Taking pictures
Tennis
Visiting museums
Watching entertainers
Weaving
Writing

RETIREMENT EXPLORATION EXERCISE

DIRECTIONS: Complete the following questions that pertain to your ideas, plans, and current beliefs about retirement. Your answers will help you understand your current feelings so you can plan more effectively for your future.

1. I now plan to retire in either _____ years, or in _____

2. At this time, the idea of retirement makes me feel:

1	2	3	4	5	6	7	8	9	10
Depressed			Neither Good nor Bad					Fantastic	

3. As of this moment in my life, my retirement planning program could be described as:

_____ Completed
_____ A good beginning
_____ Just being formulated
_____ None

4. How many people still depend upon you for emotional or financial support? _____

5. What are your greatest fears about retirement?

_____ Not having enough assets/income
_____ Inflation
_____ Lengthy illness
_____ Difficult family relationships
_____ Being bored
_____ Not being productive/useful
_____ Missing my friends in my work setting
_____ Other

6. What are you looking forward to in retirement?

_____ Freedom to do what I want
_____ Time for hobbies and interests
_____ Starting a second career
_____ More time for family
_____ Making my own decisions
_____ Rest
_____ Other

7. I think the perfect age for me to retire would be
_____.

8. I have three friends with whom I now feel comfortable sharing my concerns, fears and hopes about retirement. They are:

_____

_____

_____

9. Complete the following: "I would like my retirement to be a time in my life when…"

_____

_____

_____

_____

_____

_____

POST-RETIREMENT JOB PARTY GAME

DIRECTIONS: Imagine that you are at a party. When you walk in you realize that there are six different groups of people. You want to be with people most like yourself so you go to each group and briefly listen to them. The six groups talk about...

1. Things they did with their hands like gardening, building, woodworking, etc.

2. Crime investigations and legal research.

3. Bringing order, organization and structure to a situation that had been very disorganized and haphazard.

4. Art, music, literature and making things beautiful.

5. Starting a new business enterprise.

6. Developing a social event to help the homeless.

Which group would you pick to join first? _____

Which group would you pick to join second? _____

Which group would you pick to join third? _____

LIFE MEANING EXERCISE

Finding meaning in our lives is not a luxury, it is a need. Without meaning in our lives we would eventually get sick – the human organism ceases to operate efficiently and begins a slow descent to illness.

DIRECTIONS: Below are listed the five major life meaning needs. Try to come up with two activities you engage in right now in your life in each of these five categories.

A. Improves physical health
   1.
   2.

B. Improves emotional well-being
   1.
   2.

C. Improves mental well-being
   1.
   2.

D. Enhances socialization
   1.
   2.

E. Gives you status in your community
   1.
   2.

Please take the time to complete these exercises. I truly believe the name of this chapter is the truth... Happiness Is A Currency More Valuable Than Money. Find what makes you happy. Discover your purpose, live with passion, become self-reliant and express yourself creatively.

NEED A RETIREMENT COACH?

If you enjoyed this chapter and want to do more introspection, you may be interested in working with a retirement coach. These stimulating exercises were graciously provided to me by Dr. Richard Johnson, President of Retirement Options, Inc. Retirement Options is the leader in retirement coach training today, with a worldwide network of over 500 professionals serving individuals, couples and groups. They, like me, help people look beyond the "dollars and cents" of traditional retirement planning and focus on career, family, wellness and personal development options. For more information or to explore becoming a retirement coach, contact them at www.RetirementOptions.com

Play to Win!

"Two roads diverged in a wood, and I took the one less traveled by, and that has made all the difference."
~Robert Frost

Now that you know what you are passionate about and how you want to spend the rest of your life... what do you do next?

The answer is easy... Play to Win! I said it in the beginning. If you're working at what your passionate about, you're really playing. Now that you've got the money part figured out, you can "retire" and "play" at what you love.

People are always coming to me and wanting to make retirement lifestyle choices and decisions based upon their age or their income or the size of their portfolio. This is a gigantic mistake! Instead, you need to make decisions based upon what you really want to do, regardless of your age, and then figure out solutions, strategies and options to make it happen.

I said this in the beginning as well "Life is too long not to be doing those things that are fun and rewarding."

If you could have only one wish, what would it be?

_____

_____

_____

_____

What do you really want?

_____

_____

_____

_____

My wish for you is that the next phase and remaining years of your life are meaningful, and filled with fun stimulating activities, exploration, passion, happiness, good health, and true financial freedom. Go for what you truly want. You know what's gonna make you happy! Now, Play To Win!

Need some motivation?

*As a bonus, go to **www.MyRetirementSuccess.com**. Click on "Free Resources", then "Bill's Movies". Here you'll find **"The Winning Movie"**, my short mini-motivational movie. Enjoy it often! Please allow 30 seconds for it to load.*

AN INVITATION FROM BILL

I invite you to give me a call if you are…

• Uncomfortable with your current investment strategy and ready to make a positive change

• Not happy with the level of attention or service you are getting from your current advisor

• Looking to form a long-term relationship with an objective and independent advisor who can offer perspective, direction and guidance

• Retiring or being laid off and need to rollover your retirement plan monies

• Someone without the time, talent or temperament to handle your own portfolio any longer

I cater to discerning individuals nationwide, primarily women and couples, who crave a higher degree of personalized service, illuminating answers to their questions, and financial solutions that resonate with them both logically and emotionally. From New York to California, Maine to Florida, I am fortunate to work with a small, successful, select group of private clients. This controlled growth has been done by design so I can *personally* continue to offer the impeccable service and attention to detail that I am known for.

While many registered investment advisory firms are stuffy and indicate you must have a million or more in assets to even consider talking with them, I do not discriminate based upon how much money you earn or have accumulated. Although my typical client usually has a considerable six or seven figure investment portfolio, I have wealth coaching, advice and consulting services, and fee-only money management programs available regardless of your net-worth. I respect your privacy and will keep the personal and financial information you share with me confidential.

In order to be fair to my existing private clients and continue to provide them (and you) with the highest level of service, I have chosen to accept only 1 new private client per month. If you have enjoyed *Retire in a Weekend!* and would like to explore the possibility of working with me personally, I encourage and welcome your call during normal office hours (Monday-Thursday, 9am-4pm, Eastern) at 1-866-786-2521. I look forward to talking with you and having the opportunity to help you.

Warm regards,

P.S. When you call, if we happen to miss each other, please leave a detailed message including your phone number. We'll gladly return your message within minutes and hours, not days and weeks.

P.P.S. I work with women and couples **nationwide** and have a limited number of new client openings. Don't let geography prevent you from calling. Please phone me at 1-866-786-2521 today to explore your options!

P.P.P.S. Remember to watch the enclosed Bonus DVD - *The 10 Biggest Mistakes People Make When Retiring & How YOU Can Avoid Them!*

Recommended Resources

The 10 Biggest Mistakes People Make When Retiring & How To Avoid Them!

If you or someone you know is retiring or is within a few years of retiring, you'll want to download this FREE 30-page report! Visit **www.MyRetirementSuccess.com** and click on the report link on the right side of the homepage.

Retirement Intelligence™

Interested in enhancing your health, wealth and happiness? Retirement Intelligence is Bill's <u>free</u> award-winning newsletter delivered each Thursday via email. Visit **www.MyRetirementSuccess.com** today and <u>start your complimentary subscription</u> by entering your email address in the upper right hand corner where indicated!

Advice & Consulting

Got questions and concerns? Bill's advice and consulting services can help you make smart decisions that resolve existing financial problems and prevent future ones. For more information, call 1-866-786-2521 or visit **www.MyRetirementSuccess.com** and click on "Services", then "Advice & Consulting."

Money Management

Tired of managing your own money? Tired of poor service and lack of contact from your current advisor? Utilizing low-cost index funds, enhanced index funds and exchange traded funds, Bill's money management services may be the solution you're looking for. For more information, call 1-866-786-2521 or visit **www.MyRetirementSuccess.com** and click on "Services", then "Money Management."

Retire in a Weekend™ Retreat

You've read the book...now spend a personal weekend with Bill getting your financial ducks in a row! Your Retire in a Weekend™ retreat is a practical weekend of hands-on instruction and consulting. For more information, call 1-866-786-2521 or visit **www.MyRetirementSuccess.com** and click on "Services", then "Retire in a Weekend!" Also, please see the money-saving Special Free Gift offer at the end of this book.

IRA Rollover Helpline

Retiring? Leaving your job? What will you do with your retirement plan money? Call Bill's IRA Rollover Helpline today at 1-866-786-2521 and he'll personally handle the paperwork and rollover your retirement plan money quickly and easily. For more information, visit **www.MyRetirementSuccess.com** and click on "Services", then "IRA Rollover Helpline."

Speaking Engagements

From keynotes to half-day, full-day and more extensive training and personal coaching programs, Bill offers thoughtful and thought-provoking content that's relevant, informative, and entertaining. For more information, call 1-866-786-2521 or visit the homepage of **www.MyRetirementSuccess.com** and click on the link on the bottom right that says "Attn: Meeting Planners & Speakers Bureaus."

101Guarantees.com Books

In Chapter 2 of this book, Bill referenced his hilarious "blank" book series. You can view and order these books online at **www.101Guarantees.com**. For large quantities and volume discount information, please call 1-866-786-2521.

Contact Bill Losey

Phone:

1-866-786-2521

1-518-581-1666

Main website:

www.MyRetirementSuccess.com

Book websites:

www.RetireInAWeekend.com

www.101Guarantees.com

Movie websites:

www.TheBabyBoomerRetirementMovie.com

www.TheWinningMovie.com

About the Author

 Bill Losey, CFP®, CSA, America's Retirement Strategist™, is a highly sought-after advisor, educator and author because he makes the complicated and mundane topics of investing and retirement fun! He has nearly 20 years experience in the financial services industry and is a Certified Financial Planner™ practitioner, a Certified Senior Advisor and a Certified RSP-Trained Retirement Coach. Bill is also Founder of National Retirement Planning Month and he publishes *Retirement Intelligence*™, a free weekly award-winning newsletter with thousands of subscribers worldwide.

As a qualified professional in the areas of retirement strategies and investment management, Bill has been interviewed on the CBS Radio Network, CNNfn, Fox's "Hannity & Colmes", Bloomberg Business Radio, RNN-TV, and over 100 radio stations nationwide. He is a former guest host of "Money Matters", a daily personal finance radio program simulcast throughout NY, NJ and CT, and formerly a financial commentator for RNN-TV and guest host of the "Issues on Aging" radio program in PA. Bill was recently interviewed on the "Leading Experts" television program and currently writes a weekly column in *The Saratogian* called "Making Work Optional." He has also appeared in Financial Planning, Investment News, Inside Information, Triathlete, Senior Market Advisor, Violet for Women, Boom News, Albany-Times Union, Saratoga Business Journal, Saratoga Today, Capital District Business Review and The Chronicle of Higher Education.

In his leisure, Billy, as his friends and family call him, loves to sing. He is an accomplished vocalist and has performed the National Anthem at Madison Square Garden, the Pepsi Arena and other sporting venues. His love of singing and knowledge of money, combined with his witty sense of humor and desire to fight financial illiteracy, come full circle with his development of hilarious financial-related song parodies found at www.PerfectHarMoney.com.

Bill graduated from Marist College and obtained his certification in financial planning from The College for Financial Planning in Denver, CO. He is a member of the Financial Planning Association, the Society of Certified Senior Advisors and the National Ethics Bureau. Bill has been married for nearly 20 years to his wife Tori. Together they have three sons, two dogs, one hamster, and six fish.

 | CERTIFIED FINANCIAL PLANNER™ |

About BLRS

Headquartered in New York State, Bill Losey Retirement Solutions, LLC helps pre-retirees and retirees make smart decisions that resolve existing financial problems and prevent future ones. BLRS is an independent registered investment advisory firm that caters to women and couples **nationwide** who seek to maximize their after-tax income, reduce post-retirement risk, and generate a predictable, sustainable, increasing stream of income they won't outlive.

www.MyRetirementSuccess.com

Special Free Gift
From the Author

$1,000 DISCOUNT COUPON OFFER
RETIRE IN A WEEKEND™ RETREAT

Complete the information to the right and mail/fax us this form. We'll send you a $1,000 discount coupon good toward the tuition for an upcoming Retire in a Weekend™ retreat.

TO OBTAIN YOUR $1,000 COUPON: (There is no need to damage this book by tearing out the next page – a photocopy is satisfactory). Complete ALL the information required, then either fax this form to 518-583-9736 or mail to $1,000 Coupon Offer, c/o Bill Losey Retirement Solutions, LLC, (BLRS) 17 Sheffield Road, Wilton, NY 12831. Please allow 2-3 weeks for delivery.

$1,000 DISCOUNT COUPON OFFER
REQUIRED INFORMATION* -
PLEASE PRINT

Name

Address

City/State/Zip

Phone

Fax

E-mail address

Year you did/will retire

OPTIONAL INFORMATION - Please print

My Testimonial about Retire in a Weekend!

*Providing this information constitutes permission for BLRS to contact you about its products and services.

Notes

Notes

Notes